The Cave and the Cathedral

Books by Amir Aczel

The Jesuit and the Skull: Teilhard de Chardin, Evolution,
and the Search of Peking Man

The Artist nd the Mathematician: The Story of
Nicola Bourbaki, the Genius Mathematician
Who Never Existed

Descartes's Secret Notebook: A True Tale of
Mathematics, Mysticism, and the Quest to Understand
the Universe

Chance: A Guide to Gambling, Love, the Stock Market,
and Just About Everything Else

Entanglement: The Greatest Mystery in Physics

Pendulum: Leon Foucault and the Triumph of Science

The Riddle of the Compass: The Invention That Changed
the World

The Mystery of the Aleph: Mathematics, the Kabbalah, and
the Search for Infinity

God's Equation: Einstein, Relativity, and the Expanding
Universe

Fermat's Last Theorem: Unlocking the Secret of an Ancient
Mathematical Problem

The Cave and the Cathedral

How a Real-Life Indiana Jones and a Renegade Scholar Decoded the Ancient Art of Man

AMIR D. ACZEL

John Wiley & Sons, Inc.

Published by John Wiley & Sons, Inc., Hoboken, New Jersey
Published simultaneously in Canada

For general information about our other products and services, please contact
our Customer Care Department within the United States at (800) 762–2974,
outside the United States at (317) 572–3993 or fax (317) 572–4002.

Wiley also publishes its books in a variety of electronic formats. Some content
that appears in print may not be available in electronic books. For more information about Wiley products, visit our web site at www.wiley.com.

Library of Congress Cataloging-in-Publication Data:
Aczel, Amir D.
     The cave and the cathedral: how a real-life Indiana Jones and a renegade
  scholar decoded the ancient art of man / Amir D. Aczel.
        p.   cm.
     Includes bibliographical references and index.
     ISBN 978-0-470-37353-8 (cloth: alk. paper)
        1. Paleolithic period.   2. Magdalenian culture.   3. Cave paintings.
4. Painting, Prehistoric   5. Niaux Cave (France)   6. Lascaux Cave (France)
7. Chauvet Cave (France)   8. Antiquities, Prehistoric.   I. Title.
     GN771.A28   2009
     930.1—dc22

                                                            2009006816

Printed in the United States of America

10 9 8 7 6 5 4 3 2 1

To Miriam, who ventured into
the depths of Combarelles

Contents

Preface

One of the greatest mysteries of the human experience on Earth—if not the greatest mystery of all—is the appearance, around 32,000 years ago, of magnificent paintings, drawings, and engravings of animals inside deep and often almost inaccessible recesses of large Ice Age caverns in France and Spain (and a small number of cases in southern Italy). The art seems to have followed very specific norms: It almost exclusively featured animals; there were only a few humanlike figures, never portrayed in as much detail as the animals. There was absolutely no terrain—no trees, no rivers, no mountains, no ground whatsoever; the animals appear to be floating in space, and their images often overlap.

Stunningly, this specific practice had remained perfectly unchanged for 20,000 years—from 32,000 years ago until around 12,000 years ago; the art found in all of the decorated caves followed this exact format. Then, around 11,500 years ago, the fecund artistic activity in deep caves inexplicably came to an abrupt end. The mystery of cave art is the question "Why?"

Why would the Cro-Magnon hunter-gatherers of Europe expend so much time, effort, and resources to penetrate into deep, dark, and dangerous caverns, where they might encounter cave bears and lions or get lost and die? Why would they often crawl on all fours for distances of up to a mile or more underground, over mud and sharp stones, through narrow jagged fissures in the stony entrails of caves, aided only by the dim glow of animal-fat-burning stone candles, to paint amazing, haunting images of animals?

The discovery of the first decorated caves in the 1870s shocked the world. Attempts to solve the mystery of the purpose, the meaning, and perhaps the hidden symbolism of Upper Paleolithic cave art in Europe began after the first decorated caves were discovered in the late nineteenth century—but these attempts were made only when people became convinced that the art was authentic. (The Paleolithic is the "Old Stone Age," lasting from about 2.5 million years ago, roughly when stone tools appear—although some are even earlier than those and were made by early hominids—to about 11,000 years ago. The latter part, from 45,000 to 11,000 years ago is called the Upper Paleolithic, a period from 45,000 to around 11,000 years ago. Then comes a short intermediate period called the Mesolithic, and it is followed by the Neolithic, or the "New Stone Age.") For a long time, they assumed that it had been produced by modern-day artists, perhaps as forgeries made to appear ancient.

The first explanations of cave art were logical deductions people made by extrapolating from beliefs and practices of present-day hunter-gatherer societies, such as the magic of the hunt, shamanism, and "sympathetic magic," or drawing animals as a way to induce them to be captured. These early hypotheses were prompted by observations of modern-day hunter-gatherer societies in Africa, Australia, and the Arctic and were supported by the finding that some of the animals depicted in caves (although not many) appeared to be wounded. In addition, in very few cases, the humanlike beings drawn in caves appeared to be wearing animal masks or to have features with animal characteristics, and this reminded scholars of the shamanistic practices of some modern-day societies.

Yet it soon became clear that there must have been some mysterious and much deeper reason for the art, because the animals most often depicted in caves were not the most frequently consumed game. And the art was accompanied by strange, undecipherable signs, whose meaning was assumed to have something to do with the purpose behind this whole enterprise. Scientists were baffled; many proposed theories to explain the phenomenon, but all of these attempted explanations were found to have limitations.

Then an intellectual giant of prehistoric studies, the French scholar André Leroi-Gourhan, developed a bold theory—one that went far beyond simple implications based on a comparison with modern-day societies.

•   •   •

I became captivated with European cave art when I visited my first cavern: the famous cave of Niaux in the French Pyrenees a few years ago. Thereafter, I pursued an extensive effort aimed at solving the mysteries of this ancient artistic activity. After years of research and visits to most Paleolithic caves that are still open to the public, I became convinced of the power and depth of Leroi-Gourhan's remarkable theory, even though his writings on cave art have been criticized by some who came after him.

But later is not always better. I believe that this French expert, who wrote in the 1950s, had it right, whereas those who came after him got it wrong. It's unusual in science that a later theory should be seen as less correct than an earlier one; what is new usually supersedes the old way of thinking. But in the case of European Paleolithic cave art, I believe that what happened here bucks the trend, thus making it an even more interesting story.

This book explores the deep mystery of Paleolithic cave art—perhaps the greatest of all mysteries of our ancient past, because it can potentially tell us something meaningful about where we came from and who we are and perhaps even shed some light on where we are going.

Acknowledgments

I am grateful to Professor Alfred I. Tauber, the director of the Center for the Philosophy and History of Science at Boston University, for his continuing support and interest in my research. I thank the Center personnel and the librarians at Boston University for their help in my work of researching this book.

Many thanks are due to the French Ministry of Culture for its permission to reprint various images of prehistoric art found in French caves. In particular, Frantz Delpla and Norbert Aujoulat have been especially helpful in providing images. I also thank the Plassard family, of Rouffignac, for an image from that cave.

I thank my friend the artist Thomas Barron very warmly for the excellent drawing of *The Sorcerer* of the Chauvet cave, for the signs table, and for his deep insight into the art of the caves. I thank Ian Tattersall of the American Museum of Natural History for a discussion of cave art. I thank Julie House for information on aboriginal societies.

I am very grateful to my agent, John Taylor ("Ike") Williams of Kneerim & Williams in Boston, for his unwavering support throughout this and many previous projects, and my deep gratitude also goes to Hope Denekamp of Kneerim & Williams. I am especially indebted to my editor at John Wiley & Sons,

Stephen Power, for all of his help, suggestions, and insights into the mystery of Paleolithic cave art. I greatly appreciate the help given me by Ellen B. Wright at the editorial department of Wiley. I also thank very much the production editor, Lisa Burstiner, for her superb editing of the book.

Finally, I thank my wife, Debra, for her many ideas and suggestions and for her marvelous photographs of cave art.

1

The Adventure of Niaux

THE CAVE OF NIAUX, IN SOUTHWESTERN FRANCE, IS ONE
of the greatest prehistoric treasures of the world. It contains
stunningly beautiful art created thousands of years ago. The cave is
still open to the public, but in a very limited and controlled way.

When my wife and I visited Niaux, waiting was hard, but we
knew we didn't have a choice. Being allowed to see this cave was
a great privilege, one that might some day cease to be offered.
The cave's treasures are too fragile to expose long term to human
beings and the carbon dioxide they invariably bring with them,
along with body heat and bacteria. All of these are injurious to
this pristine environment, which for millennia has been sealed
off from the outside world. To be allowed the privilege of entry,
you must apply weeks in advance and await your turn.

So we waited in the beautiful countryside of southwestern
France, enjoying this peaceful part of the world, with its small
tradition-following towns and picturesque villages perched
on hilltops. The French Pyrenees are a rustic, heavily forested
mountain region where wild game is served in rural inns, along

with regional wines made in small family vineyards on the foothills of these mountains.

This is the region of the Cathars, a secretive religious sect that split from mainstream Catholicism in the Middle Ages. Its members were brutally persecuted by the Inquisition and found refuge in inaccessible chateaus they built on desolate mountaintops in the twelfth century. These ruins can still be seen today, dotting the lower reaches of the Pyrenees.

The Pyrenees are not quite as high as the Alps, but they are imposing mountains, steeply rising to about ten thousand feet. There are deep ravines here, and much water from melting snows flows through streams. These mountains are teeming with wildlife, such as birds of prey, deer, ibex, and even some bears, which have recently been reintroduced.

What is amazing about this land is the antiquity of its habitation: people have lived on the lower slopes of these mountains almost ever since our Homo sapiens ancestors first arrived in Europe from Africa by way of the Middle East. The oldest finds in caves in the craggy mountain slopes date from 30,000 years ago. The cave of Niaux, however, is only half as old; it was decorated by prehistoric artists about 14,000 years ago.

Finally, the guide called us. We rose early the next morning and drove uphill from the village of Tarascon, on the turbulent, muddy Ariège River, to the entrance of the cave of Niaux. The cave is situated in a thick forest above an ancient riverbed on a lower slope of the mountains.

The morning mist was just starting to dissipate as our young French guide called us to assemble. She had a tough, commanding demeanor. "Stand here," she ordered, "and everyone take his own electric lantern from the pile. Do not turn it on."

We were a small group, since only a handful of people are allowed each day to enter this primeval cave. There was a Dutchman, middle-aged and attentive; a young French couple in their twenties who wouldn't give up their cigarettes until the last moment; and then there was George, an Englishman in his seventies who had introduced himself to me at the gift shop, accompanied by his daughter and a grandson. I worried about George, since I already had an idea about what our guide would say next.

"So, remember," she told us, "you have to walk fast. We have a very long way to go underground: eight hundred meters [half a mile]. And it is on rocks and sand, and up and down. And the rocks are very, very slippery. And you cannot see very well inside the cave. Every day, somebody falls. Do you want to be that somebody? No? Then you must be careful. And do not get behind. If you do, you fall or even get lost and we never find you."

We looked at one another. Some smiled, others shrugged their shoulders. Then we turned on our lights and filed, one by one, through the narrow, jagged cave entrance. I had a feeling that our guide was not exaggerating. "Remember," she continued once we were all inside the cave, "you are not allowed to touch anything. Never ever touch the cave walls—even if you are about to slip and fall. These walls have been here millions of years, and if you touch them, you give them bacteria that can destroy the art. Okay? So let's move."

Water was slowly dripping from the stalactites above onto the cave floor, and we all started to slip here and there, barely catching ourselves from falling as we progressed ever deeper into this dark cavern. The lanterns did not provide enough light to see everything in front of us. If you focused your attention too much on the ground, you might not see a sudden lowering of the cave ceiling in front of you in time to duck and avoid smashing your head.

About fifteen minutes into our brisk march through this tortuous, dark, and narrow rocky corridor, our guide suddenly stopped. The French couple, my wife, and I were right behind her, but the Dutchman and George and his family were somewhere behind.

The Dutchman finally appeared, but no Britons. I feared that perhaps George couldn't walk as fast as required, and his daughter and grandson had to stay behind with him. Tense moments passed: had they inadvertently taken a wrong turn?

This was a very tricky underground trail. Few people traverse it, and there are no aids to finding your way: no cleared paths, no steps or pavement, no electric lighting—aids that almost all caves that are open to the public now have. There were several branching points along the trail, leading to distant dead-ends, and you could walk or crawl for miles only to realize that you were completely lost. (Judith Thurman, in an interesting article about cave art in the June 23, 2008, issue of the *New Yorker*, described an experiment in which the guides who have been working at Niaux for years tried to see if they could find their way out of the cave without light; not one of them could.) In addition, it was cold: a constant 51 degrees (outside, it was in the mid-80s). We had all been instructed to bring sweaters and other warm clothing, as well as good walking shoes, or else we would not be allowed to enter. The dampness, the constricted space, and the nearness of forbidding cave walls made it feel even colder than the actual temperature. I could see that some in our group were shivering.

Finally, we saw a dim light turning a corner in the pitch darkness of the cave. It was George with his daughter and grandson, and nobody had fallen. We were all relieved. We continued but grew increasingly tired from the exertion of constantly watching where we stepped and worrying about the changing ceiling level on this dark and narrow way. Claustrophobia was setting in: how deep underground were we now? The terrain changed frequently as we descended on a trail that was once an underground river fed by ice from the melting glaciers that engulfed these mountains in the Ice Age. Then we found ourselves walking on silt and sand that was once the bottom of an ancient underground lake.

"We must go, we must go!" urged our guide. "We have a long way still." We staggered on for what seemed an eternity, checking our every step: nobody wanted to fall and break a leg deep inside this mountain. No cell phone worked here, and I remembered the sound made by the heavy steel entrance door when it was locked behind us as soon as we had all entered this cave. It would be almost impossible to find our way back without a guide.

Our guide stopped once again to wait for the laggards, but this time she just stood in the darkness, not saying a word. When everyone finally arrived, she moved forward again and after another ten minutes suddenly stopped. "This is the entrance to the Black Salon," she said, motioning with her light forward and to the left. "Be careful, you have to turn here sharply, and at the same time walk steeply uphill. And bow your heads—it is very low and narrow here." The rocks here were very slippery, and we continued slowly. Then the path rose sharply, and the walls widened all around us. Our narrow, low, and uneven passage had given way to an unexpectedly large underground hall.

Our guide stopped. "Everyone come together," she said. "Get closer." Once we congregated around her, she turned off her light and said, "All lights off now." Reluctantly, we did as she commanded. It was the most eerie moment of my life—and probably in the lives of my companions. We stood there, half a mile deep inside a mountain, now connected to the outside world through an impossibly intricate system of narrow rocky passageways, in a darkness none of us had ever experienced. It was as if we had gone blind. We stood there in complete stillness; nobody said a word or dared to move for fear of losing his or her balance.

All of a sudden, our guide turned on a powerful electric lamp she had brought along—one that was much more luminous than our lanterns. She directed its light on the wall in front of us.

What we now saw stunned us. The light revealed beautiful and detailed charcoal drawings of Ice Age bison, horses, deer, and ibex. The stark cave wall seemed to teem with life. Images overlapped: a horse and a deer shared the same eye; a

Plate 1. Drawing of a Pyrenean ibex from the wall of the Black Salon, cave of Niaux.

bison's tail became part of a horse's belly. And each animal had been drawn in such perfect detail that it really came alive. These drawings looked as if they had just been completed by a gifted modern artist. In fact, radiocarbon dating has indicated that they were made 14,000 years ago. Plate 1 shows the drawing of a Pyrenean ibex from the wall of the Black Salon in Niaux.

Our guide pointed out details we could not at first observe. By turning her light sideways on the drawings, she made them appear three-dimensional. A bison's tail seemed to emerge out of the stone wall in front of us, and a deer's ear looked as if the animal had just turned it toward the visitor. "Notice how they used the cave's surface—the horse's hooves are placed exactly on the line where the cave wall curves outward."

"Why did they do it? Why did they come so far inside the cave?" she asked. "And they had to cross the lake, you know. It was still there when they were here, these Magdalenians. We know that, because their footsteps disappear when we get to the edge of what was once the lake." Then she said, "And imagine—they did all of this without flashlights: only carved-out little rocks into which they had melted animal fat to burn. How could they see so well to draw in such detail? And why? Why did they make these drawings?" She waited. But none of us would even venture a guess. "Nobody knows," she concluded. We stood there in the darkness for many moments, looking at these startling drawings. Then our guide turned briskly and said,

"There is more—come along." We continued, past a narrow exit from the Black Salon, walking very slowly. After another hundred yards, our guide stopped before a widening of the passageway. She shone her light on the cave wall, and what we saw there was incomprehensible.

We faced an array of bizarre symbols: rows of red dots, black lines, and designs that looked like lines with half-circles joined to them. Finally, there were what appeared to be spearheads. "We have no idea what these signs mean," our guide informed us. "People have tried to analyze them for a hundred years now—since this cave was first discovered in 1906. Nobody has a clue."

As we turned back to begin our long, slow return to the outside world, I took one last look at these signs. I was very tired now, exhausted—as were all of us—and it seemed to me that my weary, twenty-first-century male imagination was playing tricks on me: that last sign on the left looked to me like a drawing of a vulva. I must be losing my mind, I thought.

• • •

We finally staggered out of the cave, squinting in the bright sunlight. We had all survived this experience. Nobody had fallen or gotten hurt, and no one was lost. The following weeks were bewildering: my wife and I continued to be haunted by the images from the cave of Niaux. We spent much of our time pondering what we had seen: the drawings and the strange signs. We knew that Niaux was not the only prehistoric cave; there were many ancient drawings inside caves in France and Spain, mostly found within the deepest, most hidden and inaccessible parts of the caverns. The drawings and the signs were all that such caves contained: there were no indications of any permanent habitation inside these deep grottos, such as bones or stone tools (very few tools have been found, perhaps dropped by accident) or any remnants of hearths. Such signs of human occupation have been discovered only in shallow caves or rock shelters, which contained no art, and in which the Magdalenians (Cro-Magnon peoples who lived in Europe around 18,000 to 11,500 years ago) and earlier Cro-Magnons had lived.

The cave drawings always followed the same pattern: they represented animals with no surroundings or landscape, with no apparent connection to actual terrain, and rarely in relation to any human presence. These animals were often drawn on top of one another, appearing as if they were floating in space. And the varieties of animals, their positions, and their proportions seemed to be governed by arcane rules that were always roughly the same, as were the accompanying abstract symbols in caves from Cantabria, in northwest Spain, to France's Dordogne region, the Ardèche, and the Pyrenees, to a couple of isolated sites in Italy. These drawings spanned thousands of years without any noticeable change in style or subject matter. The earliest date from around 32,000 years ago (the Chauvet cave in France), and the latest are about 12,000 years old.

European cave art is mysterious because there seems to be a strong common design behind everything these Magdalenians and earlier Cro-Magnons did, but the purpose of the art and the meaning of the symbols remain a deep mystery.

After our trip, my wife and I purchased a scholarly treatise on the prehistoric cave art of France and Spain. The book contained a display of the drawings and the signs found at Niaux, Lascaux, Chauvet, and many other caves. Leafing through its pages, I suddenly came upon a photograph of that last sign I had seen inside Niaux: the one I thought I somehow understood but later dismissed as a figment of my imagination. To my great surprise, I found it displayed together with many similar—and even more explicit—signs of the same kind. Such symbols had been discovered in great abundance in prehistoric caves. And there was a two-word caption in French below the photographs of these signs: "Symboles Sexuels."

• • •

The prehistoric European cave drawings represent the first evidence of our ancestors' ability to think symbolically. These fabulous paintings of very specific animals with no background and no apparent connection to terrain or context are presumed to be symbols. But nobody knows for sure. And these totemic animals are almost always accompanied by very specific stylized signs: arrows, pairs of lines, sets of dots, and what appear to be sexual symbols. The signs may represent the very root origin of language and communication, even though we do not know how to interpret them. Their meaning is the oldest unsolved mystery of the human experience.

The enigmatic practice of creating art in deep and dangerous caves—besides the physical hazards, there were bears and lions in many caverns—lasted for 20,000 years. And then, around 12,000 years ago, as the reindeer, the bison, and the mammoth herds of the Ice Age vanished with the melting ice and the drastically changing climate, the cave art activity came to an abrupt end. Cro-Magnon societies gave way to civilization, beginning with agricultural communities and the domestication of animals in the Neolithic Revolution. The earliest writings appeared several thousand years later, and then came the copper, bronze, and iron ages. Prehistory, as we define it, ends with the invention of writing some 5,000 years ago in Mesopotamia.

Why did the cave art appear thirty millennia ago, how did it survive virtually unchanged over two hundred centuries, and why did it end? What was the significance of this unusual practice? These were the questions I was eager to address.

. . .

Niaux is one of the most important decorated caves in the world. It was not the first to be discovered—some cave art was found as early as the 1870s, such as the famous "Ceiling of the Bulls" in the cave of Altamira, in the Spanish region of Cantabria. In the case of Niaux, the first "gallery" of cave drawings, the so-called Black Salon, which we visited, appears half a mile deep inside the cavern. For this reason, although the cave had been known for centuries, perhaps only one person (who left his mark in the cave) had ventured all the way into its depths from the time the cave was abandoned some 13,000 years ago until the beginning of the twentieth century. Hundreds of graffiti have been found in this cave, but all of them were made around the entrance to the cave and certainly no more than a hundred yards inside it. The oldest dated graffito at the cave's entrance bears the year 1602.

But in 1660, a visitor named Ruben de la Vialle carved his name and the date all the way inside the Black Salon, half a mile deep inside this cavern, right next to the drawings of the animals. Did de la Vialle realize how ancient the drawings were? We do not know, and there is no evidence that anyone else had penetrated the cave to this depth. De la Vialle must have lighted his way in with fire, using a candle or a torch not much different from the kind the Paleolithic artists who decorated this cave had used.

Navigating this complicated underground network of cavities—which continues for six more miles underground in a part of the cave very rarely visited today, called the Castres Network—must have been a daunting task. And it was dangerous. We know that people have died when they got lost inside some of these deep caverns.

But somehow, Ruben de la Vialle made it alone all the way in. He saw this great art, and he made it back out of the cave. His footsteps have been found in the cave, showing his way in and out. There are also footsteps of the Paleolithic people who made the art and those of ancient visitors who entered the cave still in the Ice Age, a couple of thousand years after the artists had left. These Ice Age visitors were two women and two young children, as revealed by an analysis of their footsteps. They, too, made it all the way to the Black Salon. We know this because the cave environment was undisturbed by wind or fire or much geological erosion, and therefore ancient footsteps inside remained intact for millennia.

Once de la Vialle had left the cave of Niaux in 1660, the beautiful ancient drawings of the Black Salon were not to be seen again for almost 250 years. The artists clearly aimed—and succeeded—at hiding their drawings well.

On September 21, 1906, the Paleolithic treasure hidden in the depth of Niaux was rediscovered. That day, two young brothers, Paul and Jules Molard, were hiking in the woods with their father, known only as Captain Molard, in the rural region of the lower central Pyrenees. The boys and their father were in the habit of spending their time leisurely exploring the countryside around their vacation home in the nearby hamlet of Sabart. By late September, they had discovered several previously unknown cavities in the rough terrain of these steep hills, often by climbing with ropes on cliffs that were very difficult to reach.

On the morning of the twenty-first, they were hiking near the entrance to Niaux and entered the cave to find the graffiti in the first hall. This part of the cave had been known for many decades. But the three explorers decided to venture farther in. Rocks covered the entrance to the corridor that continued into the depth of the cavern, and they removed them, one by one, and filed through the very narrow entrance they had made. Excitedly, the two boys continued and reached the dry bed of the ancient lake, where only the Magdalenians and Ruben de la Vialle had tread, and came to the second narrowing of the cavern. Their father followed a few dozen yards behind. They climbed up through this last hurdle, and when they shone their lights on the face of what we now call the Black Salon, they were stunned to find it covered with spectacular drawings of bison, horses, and ibex.

That evening, Capitain Molard went over to his neighbor's house. This neighbor was the well-known French prehistorian Félix Garrigou. The latter, too old and frail to venture into the cave his friend had just described to him, immediately wrote a letter to Professor Émile Cartailhac, a prehistorian at the University of Toulouse. Cartailhac, on receipt of the letter with the exciting news about the discovery, rushed to the site of Niaux, bringing with him a prominent expert on Paleolithic art, the French scholar Abbé Henri Breuil (1877–1961). The pair of experts authenticated the drawings as Paleolithic (rather than present-day or at most a few hundred years old), and Breuil, who was a good artist, copied many of the drawings, which were published and roused much interest among prehistorians and the general public.

As a result of this publicity, the cave of Niaux attracted much attention, and tours were led there regularly. People marveled at the detailed art created by our Cro-Magnon ancestors and were intrigued by the mysterious signs that abound there.

But the custom of hiding extraordinary art in the deepest parts of caves, accompanied by marginal art in the periphery, and painting signs at specific locations within a cave, appears in every important decorated cave in the Franco-Cantabrian region, which comprises Cantabria and the French Dordogne (also called Périgord), Lot, Ardèche, and the Pyrenees. In the following chapters, we will explore many of these caves and will consider the theories that have been proposed to explain the riddle of why ancient peoples decorated deep caves.

2

The Greatest Mystery

I T'S THE GREATEST MYSTERY OF ALL," SAID IAN
Tattersall, the curator of anthropology at the American
Museum of Natural History in New York. He walked me to the
door of his spacious office, filled with busts of various hominids
and research manuscripts, on the top floor of the museum's labyrinthine building, on March 19, 2008.

I had been visiting Ian—a world expert on prehistoric cave
art—to discuss the meaning of the stunning paintings and drawings found in European caves and dating back tens of thousands
of years. We had a long, leisurely conversation in his office,
drinking a rustic red Sicilian wine and sampling goat cheese as
we discussed this beguiling art. Ian summed up our discussion
by saying that the meaning of this art still remains the greatest mystery in all of anthropology. After decades of intensive
research, we simply don't know why ancient artists made their
way—often crawling for miles—into the depths of caves, with
only the light from stone candles burning animal fat to guide
them through the tricky and dangerous underground labyrinths,

finally to reach the deepest hollows, where they indulged their need to paint or engrave animals.

In fact, Ian begins his marvelous 1998 book about human evolution and human origins, *Becoming Human*, with the story of the enigmatic art found in one such Paleolithic cavern, the cave of Combarelles. He writes:

> A leisurely half hour's stroll outside the sleepy southwestern French town of Les Eyzies de Tayac, a narrow fissure penetrates deep into a limestone cliff face. The path of an ancient underground stream, this tortuous subterranean passage is the cave of Combarelles I. At its entrance, a guide unlocks an ancient iron grille and swings it open . . . you proceed a hundred and fifty yards along this somber passage, wondering why on Earth you have come to this cramped, forbidding place. . . . Under the oblique light of filtered lamps, the walls of the cave suddenly come alive with engravings, some of them almost obscured by a calcite coating deposited on the cave walls over the millennia. Horses, Mammoths, reindeer, bison, mountain goats, lions, and a host of other mammals cascade in image along the cave walls over a distance of almost a hundred yards. . . . Leaving the cave, you are consumed with the question "Why?" Why wriggle and struggle along a constricted, choking, dark, uncomfortable, and potentially dangerous passage that dead-ends deep in the rock with barely room to turn around? Why create art that could only be revisited with the greatest of difficulty? Why virtually ignore the outer part of the cave, executing

your art only in its far interior recesses? Why
engrave image over image, and intersperse those
lifelike renderings with geometric designs and a
profusion of obscure and apparently superfluous
markings? And, quite simply, why the art at all?
Frankly, we will never certainly know the answer
to any of these questions.[1]

But I was determined to try to solve this great mystery.
And I knew that Ian did have his own theory about cave art.
He firmly believes that Paleolithic cave art is the result of the
development of the human brain achieving a point of no return,
a "tipping point," as one might describe it in the popular jargon: a
point at which our developing brain has made a discontinuous,
giant leap forward.

Ian Tattersall is an anthropologist and also an expert on primates, particularly lemurs: cute, furry, large-eyed prosimians
that live on the island of Madagascar. He has spent many years
studying these ancestors of monkeys, and his research has led
him to important results in the evolution of humans and other
primates. Ian looks at cave art from the strong perspective of
evolution.

He believes that the human brain is the outcome of brain
evolution that had taken place over millions of years, and that
none of the hominids that came before us—Australopithecus,
Homo erectus, Neanderthals—had reached a level of symbolic
thinking. According to Ian's theory, when our Cro-Magnon
European ancestors, members of the species Homo sapiens like
us, reached the developmental point at which they could think
symbolically, they celebrated their amazing new ability by creating art in deep caves.

At some point in the distant past, perhaps not much earlier than 35,000 years ago—the upper limit to the time span

going back into the past when the very first artistic inclination by our species manifested itself—Stone Age people realized that they could capture the image of a living thing: an animal or another human. They realized—and this must have happened very suddenly—that they could symbolically recreate the image of such a living organism.

This could have been an extension of the activity of making a stone tool. Instead of making a stone ax, the first artist of prehistory worked the stone into the shape of a human being: making a statuette (the "Venus statuettes," which I will describe later). Others may have had the idea of capturing the image of an animal on a cave wall. To celebrate this great ability, early humans created more and more such art. They reveled in their newfound ability to capture images and continued to do so for thousands of years.

It's an appealing theory, and it relies on the assumption that although the human brain has been fully developed for perhaps 150,000 years (we know this from an analysis of the cranial shape and capacity of early Homo sapiens fossil skulls found in the Middle East), something "clicked" in the human brain—some connection of neurons that allowed these people to think symbolically. Once this happened, it was a point of no return for human consciousness. At that moment, we became who we are today.

Ian and I discussed the mysterious cave of Combarelles and compared our impressions of the art found there. Right next to it is another cave that is very different from it. While Combarelles has only engravings, the nearby cave of Font-de-Gaume has multicolored paintings. Both caves were discovered by the French cleric and prehistorian Abbé Henri Breuil, affectionately known in his country as the "Father of Prehistory" (or sometimes even the "Pope of Prehistory") because, in a career that spanned more than half a century, he made so many important contributions to our understanding of our ancestors and the art they created on the walls of deep caves and on rock faces in the open air.

Breuil proposed the first theories about the meaning of European cave art. He had a penetrating eye for detail, and he had a vision. He gave us the first notions about the art, how we should look at it, and how we should think about it. Breuil made the first steps in the direction of beginning to address this greatest of mysteries.

Breuil was the first to consider the ancient art in the context of hunting. But Ian's approach is different. He looks at the remarkable Cro-Magnon cave art as a reflection of the development of the human brain. According to Ian, the Cro-Magnons produced the art of the caves simply because they could do so. It was a burst of creative energy that sprung forth as a result of the birth of symbolic thinking.

• • •

To begin to address the intriguing riddle of the meaning of the cave art, we need to understand the societies that created this magnificent and incomprehensible art. Who were these artists, and what were their lives like? Why did they create art that they hid so deep inside nearly inaccessible recesses of caverns? Were they aware that they were creating beautiful art that had never been dreamed of before their time, and thus wanted to preserve it for posterity? Were they aware of the passage and nature of time and thought of the best way to protect their creations so that future generations could discover and enjoy them? This is one explanation that has not been suggested by experts.[2]

Indeed, the art of the caverns is very old. It is the most ancient sophisticated art ever created. The oldest decorated cave known so far is Chauvet, in the French region of Ardèche, which happened to be the latest to be discovered, in 1994. The art in this deep grotto has been radiocarbon dated to as far back as 32,000 years ago.

Science names the people who created the art at Chauvet Aurignacians, because they lived during the Aurignacian period, defined as the part of the Paleolithic (Old Stone Age) period that lasted from 36,500 to 28,000 years ago. This was a time long before the Last Glacial Maximum (LGM)—the period about 22,000 years ago when the most extensive parts of Earth were frozen, and glaciers and ice covered large portions of Europe and North America for the last time before beginning their gradual come-and-go retreat (there were cold periods even after the LGM, such as the Younger Dryas, about 13,000 years ago).

The artists of Chauvet were truly ancient people. They lived here not long after the arrival of modern humans on the continent of Europe, which took place around 40,000 years ago. And yet their art seems unbelievably "modern," detailed, and alive. Chauvet is a cave that is very rich in images. Here we find a pride of smiling lions that seem in motion, hunting. There are beautiful mammoths, and there is the usual abundance of bison and horses, as found in most other caves.

The people who painted the haunting images of horses, bison, and mammoths, accompanied by strange symbols, on the walls of the Pech Merle cave in south central France lived later, around the time of the LGM, and the famous pair of mysterious speckled horses in this cave date back to 22,600 years ago. People who lived during this time period are called Gravettians. But the same cave also contains art created thousands of years later, around 19,000 years ago—by yet another culture we call the Solutrean.

The Niaux cave and the very-well-known Lascaux were both decorated by people who lived later still—between 18,000 and 11,500 years ago—called the Magdalenians. These were the most advanced of the Cro-Magnon peoples. Their stone tools show the highest degree of sophistication, and they have left behind harpoons, arrowheads, and decorated antlers and items carved from mammoth ivory.

But although they lived as much as 20,000 years apart—from 32,000 years ago (the Aurignacians) to 11,500 years ago (the last of the Magdalenians)—the people who created the great European cave art painted in surprisingly similar ways. In addition, what we know about their lifestyles, customs, and tools makes them fairly uniform. All of these peoples are named the Cro-Magnons, after the rock shelter of Cro-Magnon, in the French region of the Dordogne. The remnants of this wide-ranging civilization were first discovered near the charming village of Les Eyzies-de-Tayac. Who were the Cro-Magnons?

• • •

The Cro-Magnons were anatomically modern humans. This means that as far as we can tell from fossilized skeletal remains of these people, they were no different from us—they were a population belonging to our own species, Homo sapiens. Their ancestors, who were still Homo sapiens and hence like us, emigrated out of Africa about 150,000 years ago. They settled for a time in the Middle East, where they occupied the same caves in which Neanderthals (members of another species in our genus Homo, named Homo neanderthalensis) had also lived. Later they moved into Europe, arriving there about 40,000 years ago. Within 10,000 years of their arrival in Europe, our Homo sapiens ancestors fully replaced the Neanderthals, who by then had lived in Europe for hundreds of thousands of years.

It was through the processes of evolution that a group of hominids belonging to the species we call Homo heidelbergensis (discovered both in Africa and in Europe, near the German city of Heidelberg, and dated to several hundred thousand years ago) left Africa, their ancestral land, and found themselves on the much colder European continent—a land dominated during the Ice Ages by glaciers, snow, and permafrost. These hominids eventually became the Neanderthals.

The forces of evolution, acting on this population hundreds of thousands of years ago, produced a new hominid species that was uniquely adapted to cold weather: The Neanderthals were stout, with barrel-like torsos and strong legs. They had large noses to warm the freezing air before it entered their lungs, and they had low foreheads and no chins. The discovery of Neanderthals coincided with the finding of many stone tools, but stone tools and fossil bones had also turned up much earlier. The account of the discoveries that led to the identification of a separate, extinct human species, Neanderthal Man, in Europe is one of the greatest stories in anthropology.

Throughout history, people have been finding fossils and curious stones that had clearly been worked on: broken off from a larger rock and then systematically chipped all around to make them sharp. Such worked-on stones actually constituted various kinds of prehistoric tools used by humans and other hominids to hunt, skin, and butcher animals, and they have been found in very large numbers. These fossils and stone tools have turned up in digs and in caves and sometimes just strewn on the ground, since the forces of nature may bring up to the surface ancient layers from below the ground.

The first recorded discovery that hinted at the antiquity of man took place in 1797. That year, an English farmer named John Frere found sharp stone tools, along with fossils now known to have belonged to extinct animals, in a gravel pit near Hoxne, in Suffolk, England. Frere understood that these animals were very old and that the tools he discovered had to imply that humans were contemporary with the ancient animals that once lived in the area. He published a paper in which he described the stone tools, saying that the people who made them "had not the use of metals." But his discovery and his article did not receive the attention they deserved and were largely ignored.

In the early nineteenth century, similar findings were made, which should have indicated that humans and other hominids had lived on Earth a very long time ago because their remains or their stone tools were found among fossils of extinct animals. But none were recognized as such. The fossils were of anatomically modern prehistoric humans who lived tens of thousands of years ago and of Neanderthals.

The Neanderthal fossil finds included an 1829 discovery at the Engis cave in Belgium of cranial fragments now known to have belonged to a Neanderthal child of about three and the 1848 discovery at the Forbes Quarry on the Rock of Gibraltar of a strange-looking skull, which we now recognize as that of a female adult Neanderthal, and which was later taken to the Gibraltar Museum.

In August 1856, a great discovery was made that signaled the birth of paleoanthropology and led to our understanding that Earth was once inhabited by members of the human family who were not quite like us. This monumental discovery at a limestone quarry overlooking the Düssel River in Germany's green, pastoral Neander Valley ("Neander Thal," in German) provided the theory of human evolution with its first solid piece of evidence.

Workers in this quarry found bones and a skullcap among the debris left behind once the last cave in the area had been blasted with explosives to open it up for quarrying limestone. This was the last cave to remain unexploited, because it was hard to reach, situated on a steep ridge above the river. But finally, its time had come. Men climbed up using ropes, entered the narrow cave, and laid the explosives in place, and the foreman gave the order for the blast.

Once the dust from the explosion had settled and the workers were clearing the rubble, their spades hit an unexpectedly hard surface, and on inspection they saw a skull. Not far behind it they found a pelvis bone and thigh bones. The foreman assumed that these were the remains of a bear. He happened to know a high school teacher in the area who was an amateur naturalist. His name was Dr. Johann Karl Fuhlrott, and he had studied natural science at the University of Bonn. Sometime later, when the excavation work had been finished, the foreman contacted Dr. Fuhlrott and asked him whether he would like to come down to the quarry to collect some bear bones that had been put aside for him. Fuhlrott rushed to pick up his prize.

Fuhlrott knew enough anatomy to understand that the fossilized bones in his hands did not belong to a bear. They looked human—but not quite. The skull was more elongated and flatter at the top than a modern human skull. Excitedly, Fuhlrott concluded that these remains belonged to a human ancestor—a creature distinct from a modern human yet similar to it, an earlier human species that was now extinct. Later, in 1863, the Irish anatomist William King named this species Neanderthal, after the valley in which the fossils were found.

At first, no one believed Fuhlrott's conclusions. Anatomists argued about the strange-looking fossils, and one German professor thought that they were the remains of a Cossack who had taken part in the Napoleonic wars, was wounded, crawled up into the cave to seek shelter, and died. A French scientist, on the other hand, thought that the remains were those of a Celt with a deformed skull. Another expert thought that the bones were those of a mentally underdeveloped modern individual. No one realized the find represented anything older than a person who had been alive before the time of Jesus. The Neanderthal find was about to be forgotten.

Eager to confirm his own interpretation, however, Fuhlrott consulted Dr. Hermann Schaffhausen, a professor of anatomy at the University of Bonn. Schaffhausen concurred with Fuhlrott's assessment that the fossils represented an ancient form of humans, and he agreed to make a joint statement about the find and its significance. Following the announcement by Fuhlrott and Schaffhausen, the two men were criticized because their interpretation was considered contrary to the scriptural doctrine of man's creation.

3

The Neanderthal Enigma

THE FINDING OF REMAINS OF AN ANCIENT AND EXTINCT form of humans, called Neanderthal Man, was the greatest advance in anthropology, and it created much excitement in scientific circles. Further discoveries followed, all of which were identified as belonging to this newly defined member of the human family. These finds included one in Belgium, at Spy in 1886; several in Krapina, Croatia, in the years 1899 to 1906; and another Neanderthal fossil that turned up in Germany, this time near Ehringsdorf in 1908.

There were many discoveries in France in the years 1908 to 1914 and in the Crimea from 1924 to 1926; there were also significant Neanderthal remains found in Israel, in the caves of Mount Carmel and the western Galilee, starting in 1929, when the renowned British prehistorian Dorothy Garrod (1892–1968)—the first woman to hold a chaired position at Cambridge University—and her team excavated the Carmel cave of Tabun. Garrod's discoveries saved Tabun and other caves from destruction, since the British Mandate government wanted to turn that part of Mount Carmel—since then found to be rich in prehistoric fossils—into a giant quarry. There were finds in Italy in the 1930s, as well as in Shanidar, Iraq; and in Teshik Tash, Uzbekistan.

One of the fossil skeletons found at Shanidar was especially interesting. With the skeleton, which seemed to have been buried, scientists discovered a large amount of flower pollen residue. This led them to hypothesize that flowers had been placed intentionally with the body as it was buried, indicating that Neanderthals had something akin to ritual burial or at least a symbolic remembrance of the dead.

Neanderthals have not been found in Africa or in eastern Asia. These hominids were specifically adapted to the glacial climates of Ice Age Europe: with thick bodies, which preserved heat much better than those of modern humans, and large noses that could more effectively warm the air they breathed. They had stout limbs, and their bone fossils show signs of heavy musculature. Their daily activities included extreme physical exertion—their shin bones have been shown to withstand a stress level three times as high as the level that modern shinbones can take. Their knees and ankles were larger and much stronger than ours.

These peoples lived and hunted in the icy conditions of Europe and western Asia, using stone tools they produced to hunt and butcher animals. Some scientists have hypothesized that the Neanderthals came south to Israel and Iraq only when the glacial climates of Europe became too frigid for even their cold-adapted bodies, and during these periods they temporarily inhabited the warmer Middle East until conditions improved in Europe.

So far, fossilized remains belonging to more than five hundred individuals have been found over the entire range of these hominids. These discoveries comprise fossil bones and parts of skeletons, skulls and parts of skulls, and sometimes almost complete skeletons. Along with these remains were hundreds of thousands of stone tools. The Neanderthal's brain was actually larger, on average, than our own. The average cranial capacity of a modern human is about 1,400 cc (cubic centimeters). The Neanderthal brain averaged 1,500 cc. But how did their intelligence compare with that of anatomically modern humans? And what was the relationship between these two members of the human family?

In 1863, by the Vézère River in the Périgord, France, below a medieval rock shelter called La Madeleine, excavators unearthed a large number of curious stone tools, along with human and animal fossils. This unexpected discovery of prehistoric fossils and tools, which was made while archaeologists were digging up the remains of an eighth-century rock dwelling, led scientists to theorize a new civilization: the Magdalenian culture, a Stone Age society named after this location, which was believed to have lasted from about 19,000 to 12,000 years ago (now adjusted to 18,000 to 11,500 years ago).

The people who made these tools were not Neanderthals but rather anatomically modern humans. Such prehistoric Europeans are now called Cro-Magnons, after the discovery of the remains of such people in 1868 in the cave of Cro-Magnon, also located in the Vézère River Valley just a few miles from La Madeleine.

The Cro-Magnon people lived from about 40,000 to about 10,000 years ago, when signs of their prehistoric communities disappeared and they eventually gave way to early agricultural societies. Since they were anatomically identical to us, the Cro-Magnons possessed a chin (which Neanderthals did not: a Neanderthal's lower jaw did not have the forward protrusion that forms the chin), and therefore, at least theoretically, possessed the potential richness of our own speech. Did the Cro-Magnons have a language or several languages? And did they possess the ability to think symbolically? If they had languages, none of these has survived as such. But we do have some marvelous evidence of their symbolic thinking: the cave art they left us testifies to this ability.

Usually, caves with extensive art were not found to contain any other signs of human habitation: no fossils, no stone tools, no animal remains, and no evidence of cooking, eating, or butchering animals. The only indication that people were there, other than the art itself, is carbon remains from the burning of stone candles fueled by animal fat, which the Cro-Magnons used to light the caves while creating their art. Caves with a great deal of art in them were never used for living. And the paintings and the drawings were often hidden in the most remote and inaccessible parts of the caves.

Although nobody knows for sure, it is believed—because of the proximity of caves with art to caves at which fossils were found—that all of the art was created exclusively by the Cro-Magnons and none of it by the Neanderthals. Stone tools, however, were produced by both species, and they are similar: their type depends on the Stone Age culture to which the people who made them belonged.

The Mousterian industry (this is the term we use to describe the creation of thousands of stone tools of a particular kind that are found all over Europe) is named after the French village of Le Moustier, three miles east of La Madeleine in the Vézère River Valley, near where these tools had first been found. This industry lasted from 200,000 to 40,000 years ago and belonged mostly to Neanderthals.

Plate 2. A Mousterian stone ax.

Before and after the Mousterian industry, there were other stone industries, whose tools, such as hand axes, scrapers, points, and other implements, are characterized by shape and size; they are found in Africa, Europe, and Asia. These industries include the Châtelperronian (40,000 to 34,000 years ago) and the later ones, which I have mentioned: the Aurignacian (34,000 to 28,000 years ago), the Gravettian

(28,000 to 22,000 years ago), the Solutrean (22,000 to 19,000 years ago), and the Magdalenian (18,000 to 11,500 years ago). Plate 2 is a Mousterian stone ax. Notice its high quality and perfect symmetry.

What was the relationship between the Cro-Magnons and the Neanderthals? There is strong evidence that both Neanderthals and Cro-Magnons lived in the same territory at the same time—as late as 30,000 years ago. But the Neanderthals became extinct, while the Cro-Magnons flourished and gave rise to modern man. Some scientists believe that our Cro-Magnon ancestors caused the disappearance of the Neanderthals, either violently or by fierce competition for resources. As we will see, this replacement of Neanderthals by anatomically modern humans took place in Europe over a relatively short period of time.

The Neanderthals' ancestors are believed to have left Africa a million years ago or earlier and moved into Eurasia. Scientists believe that the Neanderthals and modern humans diverged on two different evolutionary paths more than 200,000 years ago, perhaps earlier. The record from this period is incomplete, but in a cave called La Chaise in France there have been discoveries of fossils dated to 200,000 ago, with bones that look like Homo sapiens and teeth that are clearly Neanderthal. This may indicate that the two branches in the human family diverged around that time.

Fossilized remains from a cave at Atapuerca, near the city of Burgos in northwestern Spain, were first described in a local newspaper in 1863. The complex of caves at Atapuerca has been studied extensively ever since, and at various excavations late in the twentieth century fossils of a hominid dated to 800,000 years ago were found. This hominid was named Homo antecessor ("Pioneer Man"). Other hominid remains, dated to about 300,000 years and belonging to a species named Homo heidelbergensis, were also dug up here, and they exhibit characteristics of both the Neanderthal and an earlier hominid, Homo erectus (the species to which Peking Man and Java Man belonged). These hominids were between Homo erectus and Neanderthals and are believed to have been the direct ancestors of the Neanderthals.

When Garrod first excavated the cave of Tabun at the bottom of Mount Carmel in 1929, she discovered stone tools that resembled those from the Mousterian stone industry in Europe, which is predominantly associated with Neanderthals. Two years after her find, Garrod came upon a Neanderthal skull and skeleton parts. At the same time, the American anthropologist Theodore McCown, working at the nearby Skhul cave of Mount Carmel, unearthed eight burial sites with skeletons. These were of anatomically modern humans. Some people have hypothesized that the two neighboring caves and their fossils demonstrate that Neanderthals and modern humans interbred in this part of the world. Current DNA analysis of Neanderthal bone marrow, reported in 2009, indicates little or no interbreeding. At any rate, there is proof that Neanderthals and modern humans lived very close together in the Middle East.

Around the same time, the French archaeologist René Neuville was excavating at the Qafzeh cave farther east of Carmel, near Nazareth. Here he came upon seven skeletons of anatomically modern humans that were similar to the ones from Skhul. Further excavations at Qafzeh revealed more anatomically modern humans, with distinct chins and modern-shaped skulls.

New dating of the Qafzeh cave revealed a stunning result: these anatomically modern humans had lived around 80,000 to 100,000 years ago. These dates were announced in 1980 by the Israeli archaeologist Ofer Bar-Yosef, now at Harvard University, and his colleague B. Vandermeersch. The findings caused much excitement, because they indicated that modern humans had occupied the Levant both before and after

Neanderthals did. The modern humans did not evolve from the Neanderthals.

Later, more accurate dating techniques placed the modern humans of Qafzeh at 92,000 years ago or earlier. These same methods yielded a similar age for the modern humans at Skhul. Thus, anatomically modern humans had occupied the Levant 30,000 years before the Neanderthals came onto the scene. At the same time, according to excavation results in the Klasies River in Africa, the remains of similar anatomically modern humans were dug up there. The two human species coexisted in the same region for at least 90,000 years—unlike in Europe, where Neanderthals became extinct within a few thousand years of the arrival of modern humans.

The following table shows rough dates from all of the caves studied:

Cave	Hominid Fossils Found	Age (Years Ago)
Tabun	Neanderthal	120,000
Qafzeh	Modern humans	92,000
Skhul	Modern humans	100,000
Kebara	Neanderthals	60,000
Amud	Neanderthals	50,000

These data show the clear "before and after modern humans" pattern of Neanderthal occupation of the Levant.

Why did the Neanderthals disappear, while modern humans took over? This is the Neanderthal enigma. One possibility is that this occurred as a result of abrupt changes in the environment. The world was seeing sharp temperature changes, as glacial eras gave rise to warming spells. The Neanderthals may not have adapted well to the suddenly warmer environment. They also had new competitors for resources. And they may have been killed off. Ofer Bar-Yosef believes that the modern humans' routes of migration into western Europe split the Neanderthal habitat, thus splintering Neanderthal communities into groups of fewer than four hundred individuals each. Such small communities do not possess enough genetic diversity for long-term survival.

In the early part of the twentieth century, there was still a belief among some scholars that Neanderthals were our direct ancestors. In 1908, Neanderthal fossils were discovered at the cave of La Chapelle-aux-Saints in southwestern France. The individual whose bones were found was given the nickname "Old Man," and his remains were examined by the French archaeologist Gabriel de Mortillet (1821–1898), who proposed that the Neanderthals were our ancestors.

The fossils were discovered by three French clerics, and on the advice of Abbé Breuil the bones were sent for analysis to the renowned French paleontologist Marcellin Boule at the Museum of Natural History in Paris. Like William King, Boule classified the fossil as Homo neanderthalensis, stressing the fact that it was not a modern human. Boule compared the skull of the Neanderthal with both a skull of a chimpanzee and that of a modern human in making this determination.

Boule conducted an exhaustive analysis of the Chapelle-aux-Saints Neanderthal. He made a plaster cast of the inside of the skull and, based on the relative sizes of different parts of the brain, deduced that the Neanderthal had "rudimentary intellectual faculties." Boule concluded that even though the brain itself was relatively large, the intellectual capacity of the Neanderthal was low because of the distribution of the mass of brain tissue—in other words, the fact that this distribution was different from that of modern humans (the Neanderthal skull is lower and longer than ours). Boule also noted differences in posture and in the size of the legs and concluded that Neanderthals were shorter than modern humans.

The Neanderthal mystery is a multifaceted one. Who were these people? Were they people? Could they speak? What did they use their large brains for? How did they interact with the anatomically modern humans they encountered? How did they survive together with our own species, inhabiting the same small region in Israel for close to 100,000 years? And why did they disappear so quickly—faster than the extinction of many animal species—as modern humans swept through Europe?

The February 26, 2006, issue of *Nature* included an article by Paul Mellars of the department of archaeology at Cambridge University that shed new light on why the Neanderthals disappeared. Mellars's paper, "A New Radiocarbon Revolution and the Dispersal of Modern Humans in Eurasia," made use of a new calibration result for adjusting radiocarbon dates for errors due to contamination of samples and other corrections. What the new calibration did was to shift backward the dates by several thousand years.

One result of this correction was that the scientifically estimated dates for the arrival of anatomically modern humans in Europe and their dispersal over the continent became sharper. According to the new analysis, anatomically modern humans swept through Europe much faster than had previously been estimated. They virtually took over the continent, moving at a rate of almost fifteen hundred feet per year and reached its farthest places of habitation in the Iberian Peninsula and in eastern Europe within 5,000 years of their arrival on the outskirts of Europe. According to Mellars, it took modern humans from 46,000 years ago until about 41,000 years ago to fully inhabit Europe. This rate of movement is about the same as the rate of expansion of agricultural communities, which began to spring up in the Near East about 11,000 years ago.

Although new dates for the Neanderthals should also be obtained by recalibration, it is already evident that the anatomically modern humans replaced the European Neanderthals much faster than had been earlier thought. In France, for example, Mellars's analysis implies that the Cro-Magnons inhabited the same regions as Neanderthals for not longer than a thousand or two thousand years. The Neanderthals' last stand seems to have been near Gibraltar on the southern tip of the Iberian Peninsula, where Mousterian tools—believed to have been made by Neanderthals—have been found among relics dated to 28,000 years ago. This was the latest (still unconfirmed) Neanderthal date, and it is currently not believed that Neanderthals survived beyond 28,000 years before our time. Overall, the estimated dates indicate that the Neanderthals became extinct within 13,000 years of the complete takeover of the continent by anatomically modern humans. But other analyses narrow this range to as low as 6,000 years of joint occupation of the continent.

4

The Roots of Language

IN 1989, BARUCH ARENSBURG ET AL. PUBLISHED A REPORT in the journal *Nature* in which they described their discovery of an unusual Neanderthal find from Kebara. A fossil of the hyoid bone was unearthed with the remains of this individual, which had been buried in the cave. This bone is the only one in the body that is not attached to the rest of the skeleton. It is located in the voice box, the "Adam's apple," and in humans it plays an important part in speech. Based on this finding, the authors argued that the Neanderthals may have possessed language.

Ian Tattersall is skeptical about claims that the Neanderthals used language. He maintains that the fact that the Neanderthals left us no cave art or art in any form, as did the Cro-Magnons with their magnificent cave drawings, proves that they had not developed symbolic thinking. Tattersall sees the ability to think symbolically as the pinnacle of evolution of the human mind. It is this "Great Leap Forward," as others have called it, that includes the important development of language.

Leaving aside the probability that the Neanderthals may have been able to produce some grunts and express some syllables, Tattersall and his supporters maintain that a full language was beyond Neanderthal ability, despite the fact that the average Neanderthal brain size was greater than ours. These scientists believe that something other than size was the determining factor, and that this development—unique to Homo sapiens—produced language and symbols. The Neanderthals, according to these experts, had not made the leap to symbolic thinking. And perhaps therein can be found the reason for Cro-Magnon's survival and Neanderthal's ultimate demise.

Other scientists disagree. Donald Johanson has said that whether or not Neanderthals possessed language remains debatable. Though they may not have been fully equipped for modern language, it is unlikely that Neanderthals sat silently around the campfire in their caves.

In 2000, Igor Ovchinnikov, a biologist at the University of Connecticut, and colleagues succeeded in extracting DNA from the remains of a Neanderthal baby found in the Mezmaikaya cave in the Caucasus. In 2006, the German Max Planck Institute for Evolutionary Anthropology, together with the American company 454 Life Sciences, based in Branford, Connecticut, announced that they plan to reconstruct the Neanderthal genome. Work on this genome is almost complete.

The Swedish scientist Svante Pääbo, working at the Max Planck Institute for Evolutionary Anthropology in Leipzig, has successfully drilled holes in fossil Neanderthal bones and extracted the residue of bone marrow. His team and 454 Life Sciences have subjected these samples to careful procedures to retrieve very small pieces of the DNA code, which have been painstakingly reconstructed to yield genetic information. Once this genome, now complete, is compared with that of modern humans, scientists should be able to provide us with more information about the possible genetic relationships between these two human species.

One human gene that is believed to play a role in the development of language is labeled FOXP2. Geneticists working on the reconstruction of the Neanderthal genome reported in 2009 the discovery of the equivalent of human FOXP2 in their samples of Neanderthal genetic material. Further analysis should help scientists assess the chances that the Neanderthals possessed a language.

Many scientists believe that it is not at all unusual for several species to coexist: the oddity is rather that we are now the only human species alive today. Coexistence of related species seems to be the rule in nature, rather than the exception. And if research findings about a fossil discovery in Java in 1996 are correct, then not two, but three different human species have inhabited our planet at the same time as late as 30,000 years ago. These were Homo sapiens, Homo neanderthalensis, and Homo erectus—the remnants of a hardy species of human ancestors that had widely inhabited our planet for more than a million and a half years.

By the 1940s, the science of prehistoric archaeology was advancing fast, and French and other archaeologists had successfully uncovered many remains of the Cro-Magnon peoples of Europe. The most impressive type of finding was funerary remains.

Although the Neanderthals did bury their dead, the Cro-Magnon burials were far more elaborate. They show indications of care and ornamentation of the dead, and their discovery seemed to offer further confirmation of Breuil's hypothesis: that if Cro-Magnons were so concerned with their dead, then they must have had some form of belief in an afterlife, and hence something akin to a religion. But archaeological remains of the Cro-Magnons revealed far more interesting findings.

The first Cro-Magnons to leave behind significant signs of settlement in Europe are the Aurignacians, who had greatly improved many of the earlier stone tools developed before them and specialized them into categories of tools used for many different purposes: hunting large animals, hunting small ones, cutting the flesh, grinding, and tearing, as well as making hammers and axes to be used for various purposes.

They left behind remnants of hearths and fires used in cooking food and providing heat. The earliest cave art known, the stunning drawings of lions, mammoths, and the usual horses and bison, found at Chauvet, attest to the great artistic abilities of the Aurignacians. At this time, Neanderthals still lived in Europe, but these were their last days, and they disappeared completely about 30,000 years ago, as the Aurignacian age came to an end.

It is important to understand that the Cro-Magnons lived during a period of extreme changes in the climate. Earth goes through cycles of warming and cooling because of variations in its orbit around the sun over hundreds of thousands of years. A full climactic cycle lasts about 115,000 years. There are periods of very cold winters, during which glaciers progressively cover large areas of land and the temperatures drop so that even summers are cool, and then warming periods occur. We are now at the end of this cycle, in a warm-climate era.

A similar warm period around 30,000 years ago may have helped bring about the end of the Neanderthals and the ascendancy of our own species. The Cro-Magnons of Europe did live through a number of cold and warmer peaks, and they required both warm clothing made of animal furs and skins and the use of fire during much of the year. They also used fire to help them penetrate deep caves, and here they left us their greatest legacy.

The cave painters belonged to a civilization that was advanced enough to have had a language. The effort to hunt game in a group, to butcher an animal, and to coordinate lighting in a cave required the use of language. It is therefore almost certain that the Cro-Magnons had some kind of language.

When languages die, they leave us their remnants, which are traceable in other, living languages. The examples of Latin and ancient Greek, as well as Sanskrit, as languages whose elements still live on in all Indo-European languages today demonstrate the continuity of language. So what happened to the Cro-Magnon languages?

According to a recent theory, the Cro-Magnons spoke a language similar to Basque. Basque is prevalent in some of the regions in which Cro-Magnon caves are found (along with the official French or Spanish)—in the area near Gargas in the Pyrenees, as well as in the eastern part of the coastal Spanish region containing prehistoric caves—and it is a language that is fundamentally different in its structure and origin from all other languages. It is not Indo-European, and it predates the Roman conquest of the Iberian Peninsula.

Most interesting, there are clues within the language about its origins. For example, the word *aitz* in Basque means "stone." Now, the word for "ax" is *aitzkora*; the word for "knife" is *aitzo*; and the word for "hoe" is *aitzur*. All three words for what are usually metal instruments are based on the word for "stone." This phenomenon would be very hard to explain other than by the conclusion that when these words were created, such instruments were made of stone. This would have to have happened no later than the end of the Stone Age. It indicates that when the Basque language emerged, the people who spoke it were using tools that were made of stone.[1]

But do the cave drawings and signs represent writing? After a century of intensive research, it must be conceded that not a shred of evidence has been found to support the idea that the cave drawings and signs are a written text. The cave signs may well have translated into letters of our alphabet, however. In the cave of Pech Merle, there is a sign that is identical to the letter Y. And the arrowhead associated with the bull may very well be the origin of our letter A, which came to us from Phoenician. In that language, the first letter of the alphabet is called *aluf* (*aleph* in Hebrew), which means "bull." One can trace the orthography of this letter from a pictogram of a bull's head to a stylized bull's head in Phoenician and see how it transforms into Hebrew.[2]

But despite the fact that vestiges of the Cro-Magnon languages undoubtedly exist within modern languages and some of the cave signs may well have translated into letters in modern alphabets, the signs themselves, and the drawings and the paintings found in caves, do not constitute a written text. So what do they mean?

5

Abbé Breuil

H ENRI PROSPER ÉDOUARD BREUIL WAS BORN ON
February 28, 1877, in the French town of Mortain, in
Normandy. The family was not Norman in origin but by family tradition had come from Spain, although as far as four
generations back, its members lived in the Paris region. The
name Breuil is common in France, however, and means a wood
enclosed by fences that is used as a game reserve. Henri's father,
Albert, was a public prosecutor at the town of Clermont-de-
l'Oise, forty miles north of Paris, and this is where the family
lived during the young Breuil's growing-up years.

The family, on both sides, had been in public service as nota-
ries and lawyers and some as career officers in the army. Not one,
as far back as is possible to tell, had been an ecclesiastic. Albert
was a severe man who retired early and terrorized his three children, one of whom became a lawyer like the father. The daughter became Madame de Mallevouë, and the third child, Henri,
became a cleric against his family's desire. The three siblings had
no children of their own. In 1887, Henri Breuil was sent to the

Collège Saint-Vincent, in the nearby town of Senlis, thirty-five miles northeast of Paris, in the Valois country, to study.

The school was housed in an ancient abbey that had first been constructed in the eleventh century and was run by the Marist order. The boy was not good at memorization, as he later admitted as an adult, and because he was small and frail, he was often harassed by other students. He frequently escaped to the thick forests and the tranquil fields surrounding Senlis and spent time in nature.

In July 1894, the administrators of the school decided that Breuil's health was not good enough and that he would need to take a full year's leave away from his study and do nothing. He was forbidden to do any schoolwork and spent the entire year roaming alone in the countryside, fishing, hunting, observing nature, and resting. It was during this marvelous year of leisure that he visited an aunt living in the country and through the influence of her husband, who was named Ault du Mensil, became familiar with a collection of ancient fossils kept at the couple's chateau. Breuil spent many hours in fascination handling and inspecting the fossils, which led him to decide that he wanted to pursue a career as a paleontologist.

In 1895, Breuil graduated from the Collège Saint-Vincent and enrolled at the clerical school at Issy to study to become a priest. The clerical school was located in the Paris region and was associated with the famous church of Saint Sulpice. Breuil remained interested in prehistory, and here he was influenced most by his teacher Abbé Guibert, a priest who believed strongly in evolution. "There is a lot to be done in prehistory," Guibert told Breuil. "You ought to tackle it."[1] This seems to have clinched it for the young clerical student, and he became determined to pursue a career in prehistory. He began to study many of the discoveries made in his home country about the Cro-Magnons and the archaeological remains they left behind.

Ault du Mensil took Breuil to Campigny in France, where they met Joseph-Louis Capitan (1854–1929), a prehistorian, a physician, and a member of the French Academy of Medicine. Here, Breuil dug for the first time. He identified the skeletal remains of three marmots, which won him much praise from the older naturalists.

In 1897, Breuil moved to Saint Sulpice, in the heart of Paris, to finish his studies at the seminary. Although at Issy he usually dressed in civilian clothing, at Saint Sulpice he had to wear the religious cassock, the soutane. This Italianate church is still one of the most imposing in Paris, and it houses Eugène Delacroix's famous painting of Jacob wrestling with the angel. Breuil often stared at the magnificent painting, and it was below this Delacroix masterpiece that he would be ordained a priest in 1900.

In the summer of 1897, Breuil was invited by a friend to visit the town of Brive, in south-central France. This industrial center in the Corrèze is the gateway to the Dordogne-Périgord, a French region rich in prehistorical sites. From there he went to Les Eyzies-de-Tayac, the center of prehistorical discoveries in France—most of them to be made by Breuil himself.

On July 17, Breuil joined a young archaeologist named Edouard Piette and traveled with him to Brassempouy in the Landes region. There Breuil made his first significant discovery: an ivory female figure, of a type known as Venus statuettes that is found in many locations in Europe. This energized him, and he continued on to the Pyrenees region, also rich in prehistoric sites, where he explored the cave of Mas d'Azil.

Mas d'Azil is a wide cave through which a river runs, and on its banks, Piette had found red-ochre painted pebbles, now known as Azilian, which are believed to have been painted by members of the Azilian Culture that was named after this cave. The Azilian age occurred at the end of the Paleolithic, around 11,000 years ago. Piette believed that the markings on the little pebbles were an alphabet or its beginnings, but Breuil disagreed.

These drawings resemble stylized depictions of male and female genitalia.[2] Modern science holds that they represent something symbolic, but their meaning remains a mystery.

Piette did not resent the younger man's rejection of his interpretation of the Azilian stones as an early alphabet and even commissioned Breuil to make drawings of the pebbles. These were Breuil's first professional drawings of prehistoric objects, and over the years he would make many more. Creating such reproductions would become one of his hallmarks as a prehistorian. He would follow this beginning by making thousands of copies of cave art during his life. His high-quality drawings are still used by scientists and scholars today.

On June 9, 1900, in the church of Saint Sulpice in Paris, Henri Breuil was ordained a subdeacon. But—perhaps because his family rejected religious practice—he never preached. Breuil was not interested in running a parish. He was fascinated by prehistory and was eager to follow a career as a prehistorian and to continue to make discoveries in the field.

A young ordained priest is normally sent to serve as a curate at a church somewhere, but Breuil was determined to avoid such a fate. So he applied to the Bishop of Beauvais, Monsignor Douais, who was a historian on the faculty of the University of Toulouse, and who Breuil thought would be sympathetic to his request. Breuil asked the Monsignor that he be attached to Douais's diocese and at the same time be granted a leave of absence to allow him to pursue his studies of prehistory. But the historian-bishop rejected the request.

Breuil changed venue and made a similar appeal to Monsignor Deramecourt, the Bishop of Soissons. Breuil had a number of connections at Soissons, and this helped. Monsignor Deramecourt approved Breuil's request for a four-year leave of absence from ecclesiastic duties. This leave would last a lifetime, and Breuil would never preach. Ironically, in 1947, Abbé Breuil, as his only ecclesiastical promotion, would be conferred as honorary canon of Beauvais Cathedral, whose bishop had rejected his request at the start of his career.

But Breuil never actually held any ecclesiastical post in his life, nor did he ever receive any compensation directly from the Church. He did remain formally attached, with a continuous leave of absence, to the diocese of Soissons. He continued his studies of prehistory as a student at the University of Paris and in 1903 received his license in natural science from the university in geology, geography, physics, botany, and physiology. The reason these topics were his subjects is that prehistory had not yet been recognized as a subject—it would become one through the work of Breuil himself.

Breuil had a broad forehead and penetrating dark eyes. He was short, about five feet, five inches tall, and had a slight build with rounded shoulders and small hands. These diminutive features allowed him to climb into narrow passages in caves, where others might have a difficult time maneuvering around. He had a lively and at times impatient temperament, and he looked Mediterranean, even though his family was from the north of France. During his life after ordination, he was addressed as Monsieur l'Abbé, the title "Abbé" (literally, Abbot) being the French honorific for an unattached priest, one who is not a member of a monastic or other order.

Having obtained four years' leave from the Diocese of Soissons, Breuil set out to study beyond his course at the University of Paris. He now specialized in the history of the Bronze Age, and the expertise he gained in this area would serve him well much later in life, when he traveled to Africa in 1947. He would unexpectedly interpret what he found there in terms that applied to the Mediterranean Bronze Age. The resulting theory would shock the world.

After studying early human history for some time, Breuil took up Abbé Guibert's exhortation: "There is something to be done in prehistory!" Moving into prehistory with much enthusiasm, Breuil met with unanticipated success that secured his name as a first-rate prehistorian. The Aurignacian period of the Paleolithic was named after a cave in the Pyrenees where stone artifacts had been found. This era was believed to have been part of the Magdalenian period (18,000 to 11,500 years ago). But Breuil's analysis of stone artifacts found here led him to conclude that the Aurignacian was in fact much, much older. He was able to demonstrate that this period was actually older than the Solutrean and Gravettian periods and lasted from (as we define it today) 34,000 to 28,000 years ago. By 1909, Breuil would win the "Battle of the Aurignacian," an argument about the complicated chronological dating of this period that had been raging among scholars for many years. This was the Abbé's first great theoretical achievement, and it brought him international recognition as a brilliant prehistorian. It was now his time to make more discoveries in the field.

6

Font-de-Gaume and Combarelles

IN 1901, WHILE ABBÉ HENRI BREUIL WAS VISITING THE region of Périgord with his friends Louis Capitan and Denis Peyrony (a schoolteacher he befriended in the field), the three-some discovered two prehistoric caves: Font-de-Gaume and Combarelles. These caves are still among the most important locations of prehistoric art in France because they contain extensive paintings and drawings dating back to the Magdalenian period.

Breuil was able to parlay his joint discovery into a full-time career: he studied the art in the newly found caves, published his results, copied the drawings and the paintings, and used scientific methods to authenticate the finds as prehistoric, dated to about 12,000 to 15,000 years ago. He used a magnifying glass to show that the paint was slowly peeling; a chemical analysis of the composition of the paints and their rate of peeling allowed him to make a rough age estimate. This analysis took place four decades before the advent of the much more accurate method of radiocarbon dating, which later confirmed and slightly corrected Breuil's results. But Breuil's method was surprisingly effective, and he continued to use it during his career, even after the much more exact and scientific radiocarbon analysis was developed in the 1940s.

Because of Breuil's stunning number of achievements in archaeology and prehistory and the analysis and authentication of cave art, his prestige grew ever greater. Within a few years, he became affectionately known in France as the "Father of Prehistory."

· · ·

The Dordogne region is extremely rich in prehistoric sites, whose many archaeological locations—such as Cro-Magnon, Le Moustier, and La Madeleine—have even lent their names to ancient cultures or an entire people (the Cro-Magnons, Mousterian Culture, and Magdalenian Culture, respectively). In a day's walk through the Vézère River Valley, one is likely to encounter at least a dozen prehistoric caves containing rock shelters or Neanderthal burial sites. As we will see, some of the caves in this area have been known for centuries, but the people who discovered or used them had no idea about the antiquity of their contents.

In 1896, the French explorer Émile Rivière was working in the Dordogne region, inspecting the cave of La Mouthe. While the owner of the land where this cave was found was carting away large amounts of dirt excavated from the cave's floor, the cave walls became visible, and Rivière saw on them traces of color. This was the first modern-day, recognized evidence of cave paintings in the Dordogne. The first discovery of cave art in all of France, and in fact anywhere, was made in the Ardèche region, inside the cave of Chabot, in 1878—a year before the famous (and much more impressive) discovery of the Altamira cave in northern Spain.

In 1897, a year after the discovery of La Mouthe, Rivière discovered another decorated cave in the Dordogne: the cave of Pair-non-Pair, on a cliff over the lower, northwestern part of the Dordogne region. This was the second discovery of cave art in this region of France, and the rich find of stone tools in this location raised the possibility that more prehistoric cave art would turn up here. Rivière contacted Breuil, who had again started to explore the Dordogne, and suggested that he make drawings of the art found in the caves of La Mouthe and Pair-non-Pair. Breuil made excellent reproductions of these paintings and would continue to copy cave art for the rest of his life.

Then on September 8, 1901, Breuil met his friends Capitan and Peyrony in the Vézère River Valley in the Dordogne, and together they decided to inspect two caves that were known to exist near the town of Les Eyzies-de-Tayac, to see whether they could find more cave art. The cave known as Font-de-Gaume is just a few hundred yards outside the town on the road leading east. This cave had been known for a long time, and young couples in Les Eyzies used it as a secluded place for intimate trysts. But no one had ventured deep into this cavity. When the three men entered the depths of this cave, they found brilliant color paintings of various animals. That same week, Breuil, Peyrony, and Capitan also discovered the nearby cave of Combarelles, which lies a short walk from Font-de-Gaume, farther east of town. Both caves have been dated to the Magdalenian period, but these two caves are very different from each other.

• • •

Today the cave of Font-de-Gaume is one of the most popular tourist attractions in the Dordogne (Périgord) region of France. The cave is very accessible, being so close to the charming town of Les Eyzies (which is actually a small village), with France's National Museum of Prehistory housed right on the eponymous cliff of Cro-Magnon on the north part of town and some excellent nearby restaurants that are known for local wine and delicious duck and game. . . . Since Font-de-Gaume is one of the caves still open to the public, the demand to see it is very high.

Visitors must reserve tickets for entry weeks in advance and must buy them at the small gift shop at the entrance to the gated path leading up to the cave. Fifty such tickets are sold every day for these reserved spaces. Another fifty spaces are available on the day of the visit, on a first-come, first-served basis. This results in a huge line that forms as early as 6 A.M. every day, with people standing for hours hoping to get a place for later in the day—even as late as 4 P.M., just before closing. Inevitably, most of them are turned away.

But despite the long wait and the early rise to beat the crowd and be one of the first fifty, and the return to the cave entrance at the specified time when one is admitted, touring the cave of Font-de-Gaume is very worthwhile. The visitor is treated to an experience the like of which is no longer available, for this cave is very similar to the incredible Lascaux. For decades now, Lascaux has been closed to the public because of damage discovered in the 1960s, after thousands of people visited that cave every single day. For this reason, groups that tour Font-de-Gaume are kept to a small number, evenly spaced throughout the day to minimize damage to the cave.

A steep path in the woods leads up from a riverbed to a towering cliff. Near the locked entrance to the cave, visitors must leave all of their backpacks and other belongings and put on warm clothing. Then the group files through the narrow entrance. After visitors walk for a few moments, the electrically lit path widens and gives way to a stony hall. And here, on both sides of the walkway, one can see a multitude of paintings in vivid colors:

red, black, yellow, and brown. The paintings are of bison, horses, mammoths, reindeer, aurochs (large-bodied, extinct wild cattle), bears, wolves, ibex, and rhinoceroses. It is as if one has stepped into an ancient gallery of stunning multicolored oil paintings.

After my wife, my daughter, and I visited Font-de-Gaume, entering the cave of Combarelles was a big surprise. The two caves are so close that we expected them to be similar to each other. Yet few people, relatively, visit the cave of Combarelles. Tickets for this cave are sold at the entrance to Font-de-Gaume, because Combarelles doesn't have its own ticket office, and there is usually time for a same-day visit.

But when we came to buy our tickets, we had to schedule our visit for the end of the day. Enough people still visit this cave that one can't easily choose the time of visit. Entering a cave that has been toured all day has at least one unpleasant consequence. The caves have a limited amount of air inside them, and a visitor who comes into the cave after many others have passed through it—and before the air has had a chance to clear overnight—can feel the increased amount of carbon dioxide. This results in not only making it hard to breathe, but it also makes the visitor feel even colder than he or she normally would in the cave's temperature of around 50 degrees Fahrenheit.

Visiting Combarelles was a strange experience. This cave is narrow and long, and it has some very sharp turns inside it, making it hard to navigate as one walks single file uphill under the low limestone ceiling. We had to wait for an hour outside the large locked gate at the entrance to this cave, and then our guide finally arrived. We were her only customers for this last visit of the day. She opened the gate, and we followed her in. Very soon the path became extremely narrow, and we could feel the lack of air.

My seventeen-year-old daughter, who had never visited a Paleolithic cave before, felt uneasy. But we continued on. After a few moments, we began to see engravings on both sides of the rock face of the cave. These were very densely drawn engravings of horses and bison, antelopes, reindeer, mammoths, and ibex. It was hard to keep track of so many engravings, and there was not a single drawing or painting, which made it difficult to discern what the animals were.

We had to rely on our friendly, talkative guide to use her laser pointer to outline tails and backs and horns and to pinpoint eyes. When we had gone a few hundred yards, claustrophobia set in. We felt that we could breathe only with difficulty, and my daughter was pale—I could see it even in the low light in this cave. Just when we were about to ask the guide to take us back out, she stopped and said, "I know—it's hard to breathe, and it's cold. Let's get out!" Then she stopped. After outlining so many engraved animals, she shone her laser pointer on a small engraving between a horse and an ibex, and said, "And you see this? It is a vulva." She turned back in the direction of the cave's exit. Then she added ruefully, "But without the woman."

We were eager to leave this somewhat unpleasant cave with its suffocating atmosphere. Besides the difficulties of breathing air that was low in oxygen, our eyes also hurt from the exertion of trying to see patterns in lines scratched onto a cave wall. Paleolithic engravings are much harder to make out, and they are also far less aesthetically pleasing than are the much more detailed and easy-to-view charcoal drawings or the even more stunning multicolored paintings found in other caves.

As we walked in silence through the cave's narrow stony corridor, I wondered about Breuil. How did he feel about stone engravings as compared with vivid, multicolored paintings? Did he have a theory about why two very close caves, geographical twins, really, on opposite sides of the same hill, were so different from each other? I wondered how his eyes had felt at the end of a day spent minutely inspecting and copying stone engravings, which, for us, were so hard to see.

When we finally reached the exit, we breathed a sigh of relief and took in the sweet forest air with its blessed oxygen that keeps us all alive and well. This was one cave we were happy to get out of. We decided to take the next day off: no suffocating experience for us tomorrow.

• • •

It was Denis Peyrony who had led the way into the cave of Combarelles that day in 1901, with Breuil and Capitan following behind. Peyrony was from this part of France, and he knew well the caves of the region and felt comfortable even in this narrow, long, and jagged cave. Breuil copied the art in both caves very carefully over a matter of many days.

The following year, a delegation of archaeologists came to the Dordogne in the wake of the discoveries made by Breuil and his comrades. This group further studied the art found in these caves and also used Breuil's exceptionally high-quality reproductions in their discussions. Although some stubborn objectors remained, maintaining that the art was not authentic but rather modern, most scientists were now convinced of the prehistoric provenance of the paintings, the drawings, and the engravings. Breuil would spend the following decades authenticating the art found in other caves as well, both in France and in Spain.

Several more caves were discovered in the French Dordogne that contained drawings or paintings, and all of this art was similar to that found south and across the high Pyrenees at the cave of Altamira on the north coast of Spain. Altamira was the first major decorated cave to be discovered anywhere and is still considered one of the most important Paleolithic caverns.

In France, unlike in Spain, there was less skepticism about the antiquity of the art found in caves, even among religious authorities, who might have been expected to be hostile to findings that confirmed man's existence at the time of mammoths, cave bears, and reindeer, much earlier than the age implied by scripture. It is notable that the champion of most of these discoveries, as well as of their interpretation and authentication as being very ancient, was the priest Abbé Henri Breuil. It was through Breuil's tireless efforts and his prominence and authority as a scholar of prehistory that Altamira and its discoverer eventually received confirmation and vindication after decades of disappointment and virulent attacks by religious and other opponents.

7

The Tale of a Missing Dog

IN 1868, A MAN WENT HUNTING IN AN AREA INLAND from Spain's craggy north coast, near the city of Santander, in rolling hills that were partly forested and partly meadowland. He lost his dog when he reached a high hill that had commanding views of the ocean, known as the hill of Altamira (Spanish for "High Lookout").

The dog had fallen into a small hole in the ground surrounded by rocks, and when the hunter found his dog and shoved some stones down to clear the hole so that he could release the animal, he suddenly saw an underground passage leading deeper into the earth. He marked the location of this cave, and seven years later, in 1875, a shepherd working in this area told the owner of the land about its existence. The landowner happened to be the Spanish naturalist and amateur archaeologist Marcelino Sanz de Sautuola.

De Sautuola was interested in prehistory, and he visited the cave and noticed a few artifacts but nothing spectacular. Three years later, in 1878, he went to Paris to see the Universal Exhibition. It fired his imagination, for there he saw prehistoric objects from the site of La Madeleine, which were similar to some that he had seen in his cave of Altamira. He was most intrigued by small decorative objects made of bone, such as the famous bull licking its side, a classic Magdalenian piece of mobile art. Many of the items Sautuola saw at the Paris exhibition were Magdalenian relics retrieved in the Dordogne area by Piette. Sautuola returned to explore Altamira, and it was then that he discovered the extensive cave art: images of bison, horses, and deer painted in yellow, red, and black on the cave ceiling.

In the past, de Sautuola had found artifacts closely resembling the Magdalenian objects that he later saw in Paris, so on his next visit to his cave, he brought along his eight-year-old daughter, Maria, to help him search for similar prehistoric items. When they entered the cave, Sautuola remained in the forward part of it, digging in the ground in search of ancient objects. Maria, as any curious child might do, wandered off on her own, illuminating her way into the depths of the cave with a torch.

Here the ceiling was very low, but since Maria was a small girl, she was able to stand tall and could look up at the ceiling where an adult would have had to crouch. When Maria raised her eyes to the cave's ceiling, she was stunned: she saw what nobody had ever seen before—an entire ceiling covered with red, ochre, yellow, and black paintings of bison, as well as some horses and other animals, which looked as if they had just been painted.

She shouted, "Toros, toros!" ("Bulls, bulls") and ran to get her father. He had to crawl in and then lie on the ground looking up. He was amazed. They stayed there in silence looking at majestic paintings on what is now known as the Bison Ceiling. These images looked freshly painted. In fact, they were almost 14,000 years old.

De Sautuola spent several days copying the incredible paintings on the cave ceiling. Then he sent these reproductions to the department of archaeology at the University of Madrid. Some experts became convinced that the paintings were authentic and thought that they were as old as 50,000 years—there is no reason why that number came up. When the radiocarbon 14 method was developed in the 1940s, these paintings were dated using this scientific technique, and their age was shown to be 13,540 years, with a margin of error of plus or minus 700 years.

But most people refused to believe that the Altamira paintings were ancient and rather held the view that they were modern forgeries. Sautuola was frustrated and enraged. He tried everything he could to bring scholars to the truth, but he had to face stiff religious resistance and suspicion that he was trying to gain attention for himself by forgery. There seemed to be nothing he could do to redeem his reputation or convince people to listen to him. He spent the following decades trying to argue with Spanish scholars about Altamira's authenticity and importance. People did not believe him, and he was even accused of bringing an artist to his property and having him paint the ceiling of this cave to pass it off as prehistoric. Eventually, Sautuola died a broken man, shunned as a fraud. But in France, one scholar was doing work that would eventually vindicate Sautuola posthumously.

• • •

In the spring of 1902, long after Sautuola stopped looking for recognition from the world of science and had already died, Abbé Henri Breuil obtained enough funding from scholarly organizations in France, about 900 gold francs, to support a trip to Altamira and to pay for his time and supplies, thus allowing him to make copies of the cave art found there. A local scholar, Pérez de Molina, met the Abbé and guided him through the muddy hills to the cave.

They had only candles for light and had to crawl on their hands and knees over wet rocks for more than three hundred yards underground, suffering from the dampness, lack of air, and congestion, before they finally arrived at the Bison Ceiling. There, they had to lie on their backs on bags of straw they had brought in with them in order to inspect the paintings and the engravings in this cave.

Because of the dampness, the Abbé could not use his old technique of reproducing cave art. He later wrote to his friend Broderick, "Before I went to Altamira I had never worked in pastel, but I had to do so now. The little water-color technique I had learned would have been of no use to me in the damp atmosphere of Altamira."[1]

When the weather was nice, Breuil and his associates enjoyed their lunch in the fresh air outside the cave and had a respite from the suffocating atmosphere inside, which became filled with carbon dioxide and was dangerously low in oxygen. They sat on top of the hill, from which, facing north, they could see the Atlantic Ocean in the distance.

But more often than not, storms came in from the ocean, bringing rain and mud. This was hard, tedious work. The Abbé's eyes hurt badly by the end of the day from the constant strain of inspecting the paintings by candlelight, and his cassock had acquired white blotches made by the melting candle wax. His back ached for days from his working in a contorted body position. But the reproductions he made of the art of Altamira, and above all of the magnificent Bison Ceiling, are of surprisingly high quality, and they can still be seen today. Often, they are used instead of photographs to decorate books on cave art and to show its beauty. Breuil's reproductions were published in a book that Pablo Picasso saw, which made him decide to visit the cave. Picasso was influenced by the cave art, and his painting *Dora Maar and the Minotaur* bears a striking resemblance to cave art that had not even been discovered by the time of his death: *The Sorcerer*, found at the Chauvet cave, which was first revealed in 1994.

Breuil returned to France and later took up an entry-level teaching position (*privat-dozent*) at the Catholic University of Fribourg, in Switzerland. He remained there for four years and then returned to Spain. The paintings of Altamira that he reproduced came to the attention of Prince Albert of Monaco, who was interested in prehistory. The prince supported Breuil's publication efforts and gave him a stipend that would allow him to remain in Spain and conduct further research on Altamira and other caves found in the same region of Cantabria. Like the French Dordogne and Pyrenees regions, Cantabria, too, is rich in prehistoric caves.

In 1909, Prince Albert sailed his yacht—which he usually kept docked in the Mediterranean—out through the Strait of Gibraltar and on to the Spanish harbor of Santander, where Breuil came onboard to show the prince new reproductions he had made of Cantabrian cave art. The prince continued to support Breuil's work, which allowed the Abbé to remain free of religious duties and enabled him to work on prehistoric art wherever he desired.

All told, Breuil worked in seventy-three different caves, in Spain, France, and Italy, and by his own reckoning spent more than seven hundred days inside caves.[2] If Altamira was the first of the important caves whose art was studied, copied, and authenticated by the Abbé, Lascaux was the last one—four decades later.

• • •

Although Breuil thought that the twenty superb bison on the ceiling of Altamira had been drawn by many artists over a long period of time, recent scholars have disputed this assumption.[3]

Only sixteen of the twenty bichrome animals on the famous ceiling are confirmed as bison; the remaining four have been identified as other animals, such as boars. But the bison are seen as one unit—a grazing herd. This herd, drawn in vivid colors, has been analyzed as being caught up in sexual frenzy, and two of the bison are in the first stage of copulation.

The males are often depicted as dust-wallowing, an activity that is known from observing the behavior of American bison. The stance of many of the females, with raised tails and lifted heads, has been identified as that of females in heat. The ceiling is now seen as a single composition with the central theme of a grazing, sexually charged herd of bison. These figures are large, each about four to five feet in length, and they span the cave ceiling in various places, as is often seen in other caves, but the animals' positions are all believed to be perfectly correlated with one another. This is a symbolic conception of an entire group of animals acting as a unit, and recent analysis shows clear male-female associations in this integrated composition. The portrayal is also identified as a seasonal depiction, because European bison are known to rut in August and September.[4]

The horse is the main opposing animal on the great ceiling. It is also drawn in bichrome, red and black, and it stands in contrast to the rutting herd of bison. There is a large hind on the other side, on the periphery of the ceiling. This is an accompanying animal to the main theme of the ceiling, but it is drawn in a size larger than that of a bison. In the corridor outside the Great Hall are engravings of bison and mammoths, which are also accompanying animals of the bison in the main theme of the ceiling composition.[5]

Even some earlier observers have noted the seeming unity of the paintings on the ceiling at Altamira and their unique qualities. There is a good reason this cave was dubbed the Sistine Chapel of prehistoric art.

8

The Sign of the Bull and the Legend of the Minotaur

SOON AFTER THE DISCOVERY OF THE FIRST CAVES IN France, Font-de-Gaume and Combarelles in 1901 and Niaux in 1906 (the art of which has also been studied, copied, and authenticated by Abbé Henri Breuil), scientists began to address the deep mystery of the meaning of the myriad signs that invariably accompany the glorious art in these caves.

A commonly occurring sign in some decorated caves in France and Spain, such as Niaux and Altamira, is the arrowhead:

This particular sign is almost always associated with the bison or the wild ox. Sometimes it appears right next to the bison (either male or female, from what experts can tell), and sometimes it is embedded in the flank, the back, or the shoulder of the animal. Other animals may have other signs associated with them, but it seems that the arrowhead was reserved for the bison and the aurochs. This observation was the first bit of progress that was made in trying to decipher what the signs mean.

Breuil developed a theory about cave art. He believed that the purpose of the art was something akin to a religious ritual. According to this view, the Cro-Magnon artists drew and painted the animals they hunted as a form of prayer: the drawing of the animal was a prayer to God, or gods, to bring success in the hunt. The most common sign that Breuil saw in the caves, an arrowhead associated with the bison, was interpreted as a visual symbol of the plea to God for help in hunting this animal with spears or arrows—implements that were represented by the arrowhead sign.

Breuil's interpretation made much sense at that time, especially given the prevailing religious fervor among certain segments of society during this period, and many people embraced it. It seemed as if we were getting closer to under-standing the true meaning of the art and its purpose. The prehistoric cave artists were seen as members of hunter-gatherer societies that depended on the hunt for their survival, and they specialized in this form of prayer to speed the hunt for food. The artists were priests who served the hunting community.

The appearance of paintings and drawings that included only animals was seen as a confirmation of this priestly hypoth-esis. Since the hunters cared only about finding the animals themselves, there was no need for the artists to paint or draw any terrain. Mountains, rivers, hills, trees, rocks—all of these were unnecessary, and hence were left out. The purpose of the art was to ensure a good hunt, and, therefore, only the animals were depicted. The sign of the arrow, associated with a wild bull or a bison, represented the weapon by which the animal would be hunted. Depicting both weapon and prey superimposed on a wall of a deep, primeval cave was man's prayer for success in the continuing hunt of this large animal. It seemed, then, that the mystery was solved, and Breuil's prestige grew even greater.

But the signs found in caves appear in very well-defined sets and categories: they are not random, and they include many more elements than what looks like an arrowhead. The arrow is only one of many mysterious notations drawn or carved on the limestone or granite walls of deep caves.

And even though these signs and the art they accompany span 20,000 years—from around 32,000 years ago to about 12,000 years before the present—they are fairly uniform: much more uniform and homogeneous than one might expect, given such a vast time span and geographical spread.

The French scholars André Leroi-Gourhan and Annette Laming-Emperaire have recognized two kinds of signs in caves: wide signs and narrow ones. In the cave of Pech Merle and in the nearby cave of Cougnac, for example, there are very similar signs that are wide, and hence similar to the arrow sign. In Chauvet (to be discovered long after the work of these experts), there is a sign resembling the letter W. This, too, is a wide sign. The following are wide signs:

At other locations within some caves are found narrow signs. Shown below are some examples of narrow signs:

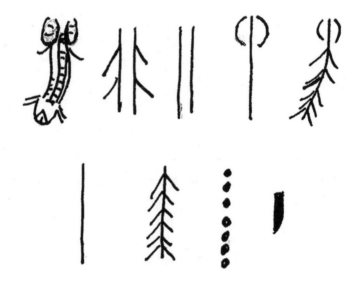

Having made the useful classification into narrow and wide signs, French scholars realized that what they had found was meaningful. Every new sign they analyzed seemed to fall nicely into one of the two categories, with little ambiguity. The next step was to develop a theory of what these signs actually meant. Laming-Emperaire and Leroi-Gourhan made a considerable advance here, which I will discuss later.

But the sign of the bull and the ubiquitous images of bulls themselves apparently had great significance in the Paleolithic. And there is a possibility that the idea behind this preoccupation with bulls, their signs, and whatever symbolism they carry in the human mind transcended this era and progressed with human civilization out of the Paleolithic and into the agricultural settlements of the Neolithic and beyond to the Bronze Age.

The bull images of the Magdalenians, as seen on the ceiling of Altamira and the walls of so many Paleolithic caves in France and Spain, may well have morphed into bull images that were prevalent in Neolithic settlements in Western Asia: the Jordan Valley, the Syrian Plateau, and southern Anatolia. These images of bulls, present in great numbers and over a large geographical region, bear witness to what archaeologists have named a Cult of the Bull.

The Neolithic settlements, which began to be established in the Middle East after the end of the Magdalenian period in Europe, around 11,000 years ago, consisted of primitive buildings and worked fields—the very beginnings of agriculture. In Jericho, considered the oldest "city" in the world, a fortification tower was discovered, measuring twenty-five feet in height and attached to a thick wall. This was a large agricultural community that thrived around 11,000 years ago. Continuing settlement at this location makes it the oldest existing city from the Neolithic to the present day. The agricultural settlers who lived here during the Neolithic period seem to have worshipped the bull. This is evidenced by the remains of wild cattle found under buildings. But stronger archaeological evidence for this assertion was found at other locations in the Middle East and Anatolia.

The people of the Neolithic no longer lived in caves, rock shelters, or open light structures on the land, and they did not enter deep caverns to draw pictures. Instead, they drew and painted images on the walls of their houses. In both of these geographical areas there are paintings of bulls on walls, and archaeologists have conjectured that there existed a cult that worshipped or admired the bull.

• • •

In the southern part of the Anatolian plateau, in a place called the Konya Plain, is the site of a Neolithic town, named by archaeologists for the nearby Turkish settlement of Çatalhöyük, which was occupied around 9,000 years ago. This ancient settlement was established when agriculture came to Anatolia from its inception in the Middle East, in the Jordan Valley around 11,500 years ago. The town of mud bricks and stone was built in such a way that all of the houses were touching, their outer walls forming a formidable wall around this entire Neolithic settlement, without an obvious entrance. It's a big site—around thirty-two acres in total—so this was a considerable-size town that subsisted with the earliest type of agriculture and animal domestication.[1]

When the English archaeologist James Mellaart, of the British Institute of Archaeology in Ankara, first came to the Konya Plain in November 1958 looking for an interesting site to dig, he saw an imposing wide mound and decided to excavate. He had no idea what he was getting into. The Çatalhöyük site was so large that in many years he had been able to unearth only a part of it. But what he found at Çatalhöyük stunned the world.

The excavators discovered entire dwellings: houses made of mud and stone built nine millennia ago. Painted on the inside walls of every house were large, imposing frescos of bulls. As the archaeologist Steven Mithen described in his book *After the Ice*, in one house there was a "monstrous scene of bulls bursting from the wall. There were three of them at waist height, white heads striped with black and red, with enormous pointed horns that seem to threaten human life within the room."[2]

There were signs here as well—just as in Paleolithic caves in France and Spain—associated with the bulls. These were geometrical designs and handprints in black and red, similar to those found in the cave of Pech Merle, which had been created by Paleolithic artists 11,000 years earlier, around 20,000 years ago. According to Mithen, a visit to Çatalhöyük brings one to "a nightmare vision of the world that farming has brought to these particular members of humankind."[3]

It is believed that in every room at Çatalhöyük, people kept clay figurines—mostly of women—that they placed in niches in the walls. One of the statuettes found here was of a woman sitting on a throne, flanked by two leopards; she has a hand on each leopard's head, and their tails are wrapped around her body.[4]

The bulls vary from room to room, but they always seem menacing: they have large heads with long, twisted horns aimed at the viewer, and their faces are covered with strange markings. In one house, bulls' heads stretched from floor to ceiling; in another were stone pillars with bulls' horns on them.

Geometrical designs appeared everywhere, and some rooms featured paintings of large black vultures attacking people without heads. In one house, there were clay-and-plaster sculptures of women's breasts, with the nipples stripped off to reveal the skulls of vultures, foxes, and weasels inside.

Further study of the site by the English archaeologist Ian Hodder, who had been Mellaart's student in England and who later became a professor at Cambridge, determined that the walls of the rooms had as many as forty layers of paint and plaster. It seemed that these walls and frescos had been repainted every year—or every time someone died and was buried under the floor of the room, as was the custom of the strange people who lived here so long ago.

According to Hodder, ritualistic and domestic activities at Çatalhöyük took place simultaneously. Mithen stated, "To me it seems as if every aspect of their lives had become ritualized, any independence of thought and behavior crushed out of them by an oppressive ideology manifest in the bulls, breasts, skulls, and vultures."[5]

There was clearly some version of the Cult of the Bull at Çatalhöyük, as was indeed also found in sites in the Middle East, such as Ain Ghazal, in Jordan, where clay figurines of wild cattle turned up, and at Mureybet, in northern Syria, where human female figurines, as well as stone carvings and buried skulls and horns of wild bulls, were found under floors of buildings in a Neolithic settlement dated to 11,000 years ago. It even appears that skulls of wild oxen once hung on walls here.[6]

Later, during the Bronze Age in Minoan Greece, the Cult of the Bull morphs into the legend of the Minotaur. According to Greek mythology, the Minotaur was a creature that was half-bull and half-human—he was born of the union between Pasiphaë, the wife of King Minos of Crete, and a wild bull given to Minos by Poseidon. The god of the sea had intended Minos to sacrifice the bull to him, but Minos couldn't do it because the bull was too beautiful. To punish Minos for his refusal, Poseidon made Pasiphaë fall in love with the bull and give birth to the Minotaur. When the Minotaur was born, Minos had the architect Daedalus build the Labyrinth: an impossibly complex maze of underground interconnected chambers and pathways, from which escape was supposed to have been impossible. Young Athenians were brought to the Labyrinth to fight the Minotaur, perhaps in a way that later led to Spanish bullfighting.

One cannot escape the feeling that the idea for the Labyrinth was a reflection—perhaps a folk memory—of the endless connected halls and passageways one finds inside a decorated Paleolithic cave in France or Spain, and these caverns were most often covered with drawings, paintings, and engravings of wild bulls.

The site of Knossos, on the northern coast of Crete, had been a Neolithic settlement dated to about 9,000 years ago—not too long after the end of the Magdalenian age in France and Spain. At the same location was found the palace of the actual King Minos of Crete, about whom the mythological legend of the Minotaur was imagined. The discovery of the palace took place in 1900, when the British archaeologist Arthur Evans excavated the site.

Evans was one of the greatest—and most controversial—archaeologists. He was untrained in the field but was wealthy. He purchased the land where he thought he might find the real city of King Minos. He hired hundreds of local people to work on the site, and he succeeded in his quest. In March 1900, Evans and his team discovered the palace on which the myth was based. This was a maze of more than a thousand rooms, and it resembles the mythological description of the Labyrinth. Artistic motifs here, especially a double ax that resembles a pair of horns, are suggestive of a bull.

Evans was controversial because he was the first archaeologist to reconstruct the ruins he discovered. Not only did he rebuild any broken structures he uncovered, but he even painted surfaces in what he thought were the original colors of the time. The palace of Knossos—King Minos's abode—was built around 1700 BC, with some structures predating it. The thriving culture on Crete and other Aegean islands of that time is called Minoan, after King Minos. At about 1628 BC, the palace, including the labyrinthine rooms that gave rise to the legend, and the surrounding walls and habitations associated with the Minoan civilization, were all destroyed by the eruption of the volcano on the nearby island of Santorini (also called Thera), which itself had a Minoan city with many buildings, streets, and flushing toilets in houses. The sudden destruction of such an advanced, thriving Bronze Age civilization gave rise to another legend: Atlantis.

The legend of the Minotaur may well be a continuation of the bull images from Paleolithic caves through the Neolithic connection on Crete. The strange Neolithic Cult of the Bull, the Greek mythological stories about bulls and mazes and creatures that were half-human and half-bovine, and even modern-day bullfighting may all have originated, through human consciousness and storytelling, in Paleolithic cave art.

9

Rouffignac and Pech Merle

PREHISTORY AND PALEOANTHROPOLOGY WERE NEW sciences at the turn of the twentieth century, and people who left their mark on the study of our ancestors were not necessarily those who had good scientific training, but rather people who had done good field work. Abbé Henri Breuil was by far the most experienced scientist in this area. In 1915, after paintings in the cave of Rouffignac came to light in the Dordogne region, Breuil was there.

He crawled on all fours underground for more than half a mile—the cave ceiling was extremely low—and when he arrived at the "Deep Gallery" of this cave, he found a breathtaking display of drawings of mammoths (which made this cave famous), as well as bison, horses, deer, and ibex. By now, Breuil was the undisputed expert on prehistoric cave art in France, and his word carried weight in scientific circles.

The cave of Rouffignac, whose entrance is at the top of a high hill in the Dordogne, northwest of Les Eyzies, is very deep. This cave is different from all of the others in that it is so deep that visitors would find it difficult and, above all, claustrophobic if they were to walk into its depths. Rouffignac therefore has an electric train inside it, to carry passengers all the way down to its celebrated Deep Gallery (Galerie Profonde, in French).

The administrators of this cave also claim that the train helps prevent damage to the prehistoric site by keeping visitors onboard, rather than allowing them to wander off on their own, where they might touch the sensitive cave walls. More important, the administrators claim, transporting visitors by train keeps them from exerting themselves, which would create much more carbon dioxide than when people remain stationary on a moving train.

• • •

My wife, my daughter, and I boarded the train just inside the entrance to the cave, and, as usual, the steel door was locked behind us. We climbed onto the open train cars, the electric locomotive pushed off, and we started our descent. We rolled down steep tracks into the rather unpleasant depths of a musty, dusty cave. Human beings are inclined to dislike going down into the unknown bowels of the earth, and we wished that we could stop somewhere.

But the route ahead of us was long. After we rode down a sharp decline for about fifteen minutes, the guide stopped the engine. He turned on his flashlight and shone it on the cave wall. We saw an enchanting drawing of a pair of mammoths that looked real, as if they had just been sketched by a modern artist. We admired this drawing for a short while, and as we continued down, farther and farther into the depths of the cave, we stopped a few more times to see other isolated drawings of rhinoceroses and horses. But the main attraction was at the bottom of this endless cavern, very deep inside the massive mountain.

Farther down, we stopped in front of an array of signs, which were mostly dots arranged in various ways. This was an "indicative panel," which generally shows that a major gallery is coming up ahead. French guides who work for the authorities that administer Paleolithic caves in France are very knowledgeable. They keep up with the literature; they read new research, and they often have very interesting information on the latest scientific findings. Our guide tried to interpret for us the mysterious indicative panels on cave walls that appeared just before the main galleries. He described some of these elements as "ethnic signs," akin to tribal insignia or artists' signatures. It's an interesting theory held by certain experts on cave art, and it has some appeal: we see signatures on canvasses or watercolors, statues, and even a few oriental rugs. If your medium is a rock face a dozen or more millennia ago, why wouldn't you sign your name on a nearby rock panel—or mark the symbols of your tribe or family group?

We continued our deep descent and finally entered a chamber with no exit other than the way we had come down. We had reached the very end of the line—the Deep Hall—and here we disembarked from the train and gathered around our guide. This gallery is smaller than most, and it is low. In that sense, it resembles Altamira: the drawings are on the ceiling. But what a ceiling this was!

We stood there, crowded together in a tiny hall at a depth we could not even imagine. The air was of poor quality—it smelled heavily of dust and mustiness and chalk and limestone. It was hard to breathe. Our guide shone his light on the magnificent ceiling, speaking rapidly in French with an accent that reflected the dialect of this remote rural area. At times, it was hard to understand. But the drawings spoke for themselves.

It was clear that a very thoughtful artist or artists had planned out the entire display even before beginning the work. There was no color here; everything was drawn in black. Deer, ibex, and mammoths were arranged in a circular fashion all around the ceiling. And even without any terrain, they seemed to be prancing around. These animals looked as if they were smiling—they reminded me of the painting *The Peaceable Kingdom* by Edward Hicks, except that there were no humans in the Rouffignac composition, only animals. Plate 3 shows part of the impressive Grand Ceiling of the cave of Rouffignac.

What was also stunning about this display was the way the art had been created. Before the train tracks were put in, the cave floor was dug out to a depth of ten feet or more. Originally, the passage into this cave was so shallow that a person could not walk upright. When Breuil came here decades ago, he had to crawl on all fours for *half a mile* inside this cave to reach the Deep Gallery. There, he had to lie on his back to inspect and copy the drawings from the ceiling. How he could accomplish this without succumbing to claustrophobia and lack of air is a modern mystery. And we know that this cave was dangerous.

Plate 3. Mammoth and ibex on the Grand Ceiling of the cave of Rouffignac.

People have known about the cave of Rouffignac for a very long time. The first record of its exploration goes back to 1575, in the writings of Françoise de Belleforest—one of the first speleological descriptions in history. Early visitors, Belleforest and those who followed in the coming centuries, saw some of the art in this cave, because it begins close to the entrance. But it is unlikely that any of these cave explorers understood that what they were viewing had been created 15,000 years ago.

In 1715, the famous Marquis de Miremont wrote a comprehensive description of the topography of the cave, and in 1759,
Gabriel Bouquiet published the first detailed map of the cavern.
The map, unfortunately, was not published early enough. In
1730, two visiting speleologists from Holland explored the cave
and lost their way in it. After some time, they ran out of fuel
for their fire. To keep the fire going, they burned their clothes.
Still, they could not find their way out. Within a few days, one of
them died. The second man continued to search in the dark for
nine days before finally finding the entrance. But by the time he
emerged from Rouffignac, his health had deteriorated so much
that within two days he died.

This tragic incident testifies to how dangerous the caves
must have been in prehistoric times, when the Cro-Magnon
painters spent days in the inner recesses of these caverns and
found their way around with fewer aids than were available in
the eighteenth century. (The compass, for one, was invented
in the twelfth century.)

• • •

In 1922, another decorated cave was discovered in France. This
one was neither in the Périgord nor in the Pyrenees. It was
found in the department of Lot, some miles northeast of the
town of Cahors, on a mountain with the mysterious name of
Pech Merle. The name is derived from the dead Occitan language, which was spoken in parts of southern France in the
Middle Ages. *Pech* means "hill" in Occitan, but the meaning of
Merle is unknown.

Two children came across the cave entrance by chance
while walking in the wooded hills above the little village of
Cabrerets, and they entered it. Sixteen-year-old André David and

fifteen-year-old Henri Dutertre brought their discovery of the strange black-and-red paintings deep inside the cave to the attention of Amédée Lemozi, the priest of Cabrerets. Lemozi, who was also an amateur prehistorian, began to study this curious, fascinating art, and he involved the entire village in the findings.

The village of Cabrerets took pride in the cave it owned and in 1926 opened it to the public. To this day, tourism to the cave of Pech Merle is a brisk industry, owned and operated by Cabrerets and bringing in hundreds of visitors every day. But the number of people allowed into the cave daily is limited to seven hundred, to minimize damage to the delicate paintings. The cave's entrance had been closed naturally in mud slides following the massive melting of the glaciers at the end of the Ice Age, and the cave had not been entered since then, until its serendipitous discovery in 1922.

Some of the art inside the Pech Merle cave was radiocarbon dated to 22,600 years ago (the famous pair of horses), and other sections are a few thousand years younger. There are drawings of mammoths and rhinoceroses here, as well as the usual bison. Many sexual signs appear as well, along with stylized drawings of naked women that resemble the Venus statuettes found at prehistoric archaeological sites. But in the deepest hall within this cave is one of the most haunting prehistoric drawings ever discovered. It consists of an abstract depiction of two horses. The horses were drawn using red dots. Their heads and legs are diminutive; their backs are massive. This cave painting could be seen as an ingenious prehistoric pointillism. Plate 4 shows the dotted horses of the cave of Pech Merle.

Plate 4. The dotted horses of the cave of Pech Merle.

The rough surface of the stone wall on which the horses were drawn was used in the drawing: the head of the right horse is outlined by a broken rock in the shape of a horse's head but is reflected in a smaller head for the same animal, drawn in black. The second horse has only one black head. On the back of the right horse is a large fish, identified as a pike. But most puzzling of all: symmetrically placed around this mysterious drawing are the black imprints of six hands.

. . .

The distance to be traveled to Pech Merle from Sarlat, a town larger than Les Eyzies but still in the Dordogne, was not long, as seen on a map. Pech Merle is in another department, the Lot, on the east side of the main highway running down from Paris to the south of France, the A20. I sped down the autoroute and took the exit by Cahors, a medieval town with a historic bridge over a river, which is known for the excellent wines made in this area.

I turned off at the exit and took the small curvy road, the D662, then wound my way east toward the picturesque village of Saint Cirq Lapopie. After an hour of turns on this narrow road, barely dodging oncoming traffic, I reached the turnoff to the left, which took me up the limestone cliffs to the tiny village of Cabrerets. At the very top of the hill was a large, dusty parking lot, and I proceeded to the cave's entrance to buy my ticket.

The guide, a young man who spoke only French, gave everyone printed pages explaining the paintings we were about to see, in whatever language the visitor might speak, even Hebrew and Japanese. He led us down the steep staircase into the cave and locked the door behind us. The Pech Merle cave is different from almost every other decorated cave I have visited because it is not a narrow passage that continues for half a mile or more before opening into wide galleries. This cave is one self-contained large hall consisting of various levels. Visiting Pech Merle, one walks around the immense underground hall in a circular fashion, going down several levels, then climbing up and completing a circle that brings one back to the entrance. This much more open structure makes Pech Merle the least claustrophobic cave I've ever visited.

When I entered the cave, the first thing I saw was the roots of a huge oak tree that was growing outside, above the cave. These thick roots hung down forlornly from the cave ceiling and made for an eerie reminder that I was now in the underground world below the surface of the earth—I was inside a subterranean labyrinth among the sinuous roots of trees. And then I descended farther.

As I proceeded into the depths of the cave, I saw the usual stalagmites and stalactites, some still dripping water. At one place near these stalactites were natural beads that looked like perfect little spheres. No one knows exactly how they were formed. As I continued on with my group, we came across bison, horses, and mammoths painted red. But there were also stylized feminine human figures—such as the one shown below, from Pech Merle.

Such stylized depictions of women are believed to fall in a category somewhere between a drawing and a sign. In fact, many signs found in caves can be considered further abstractions of the female drawings of Pech Merle. The French call such symbols *claviform signs*, and they can be seen in the table of signs on page 79.

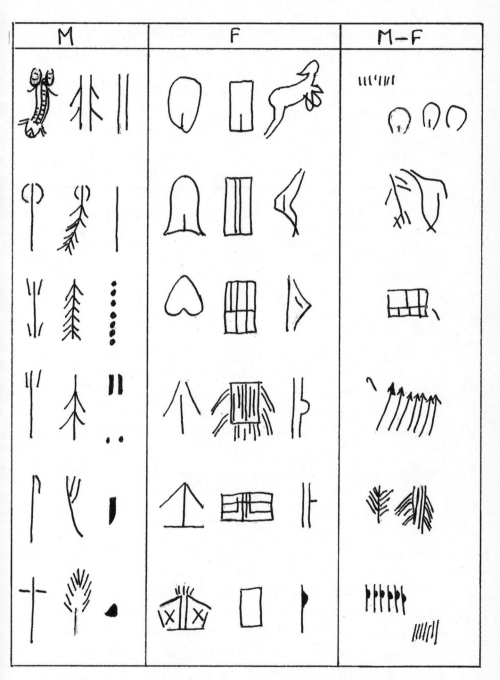

Claviform signs, right column of set F, in Thomas Barron's table of signs.

As we progressed, we passed from niche to niche, where we saw various painted or drawn animals. Then we came to the lowest level of Pech Merle, which contains the masterpiece of this entire cave: the famous dotted horses. The location and the use of the rock on which the pair of horses is drawn are believed to be symbolic. The horses point to the cave's entrances, and the prehistoric artists made special use of the particular surface of the rock. The right horse's head is composed of the outline of the rock itself. But the ingenious artist who created the horse also gave it a much smaller painted head, as if reflecting the shape of the head made by the natural rock. We stood speechless next to this masterpiece, then we continued toward the exit.

• • •

Paleolithic cave artists were very creative and had mastered their techniques amazingly well. To light their way into the caves and provide lighting while they made their artwork, Paleolithic artists invented stone candle holders. These were palm-size rocks that had been cut or chiseled, in a way similar to that of producing stone axes, so that both sides were convex-shaped: the bottom was round, and the top had a round hollow carved out of it. This stone cup held a lump of animal fat, into which a straw wick was placed. Once lit, the candle produced light for many hours.

The cave artists used sharp stone tools to carve images on cave walls, as well as brushes made of plants to draw and paint images. They blew wet paint through hollow reeds onto cave walls in order to fill areas and sometimes to stencil hand imprints on walls. They used their fingers and palms to plaster walls with paint to make signs, as well as printed hand images. The dots on the horses of Pech Merle are fingerprints.

The Paleolithic masters were adept at finding colored pigments in their environment. Burned pinecones and branches were used to make charcoal. Fortunately for posterity, the charcoal images are not only of lasting quality, but because they are based on carbon, they can be carbon-dated with great precision (it was thus that the horses of Pech Merle were dated to 22,600 years ago, with a "standard error"—a measure of how far away from this number the actual age may be—of only about 500 years). Compounds of manganese and other metals provided the artists with other colors. They used red ochre as often as charcoal, and two other common colors were yellow and brown, produced from various minerals found in the ground. The pigments were mixed in a water solution that was held in a stone cup similar to those used for lighting.

The artists seem to have understood perspective—an incredible achievement for people living more than twenty millennia ago. And the horses of Pech Merle attest to the invention of pointillism a thousand generations before our time. Art historians have been baffled by how much our distant ancestors knew about art and how to create it.

The choice of cave terrain to paint the "canvasses" of prehistory seems to have been made with equal care as the art itself. In the case of the beautiful pair of horses, a vertical rock slab had detached itself from the wall of Pech Merle in a primeval earthquake eons ago, and one can almost hear the thoughts of the prehistoric Picasso as he considered it the perfect surface to paint on: "The corner looks like a horse's head. . . . Let me turn this into a pair of horses, intertwined, with the rock head reflected in a smaller head I will draw." Then he added a fish on one of the horses' backs and decorated it with fingerprints and hand stencils.

In other cases, the choice was not always obvious. The surface of the rocky cave wall was always used in one way or another—to add depth perception, to aid in perspective, or to add natural lines to an animal. The general rules based on the importance of the location rarely seem to have been violated: Place your best artwork in the depths of the cavern, with accompanying creations around it, and allow novices to practice on walls that are close to the cave entrance—these seem to have been deemed less important. Finally, place your signs in strategic "indicative panels" that lead to your masterpieces.

10

The Discovery of Lascaux

A DOG THAT WENT MISSING HAS FIGURED IN THE discovery of at least one other cave—and one that has equaled Altamira in importance and surpassed it in fame. On Thursday, September 12, 1940, two teenagers named Marcel Ravidat and Jacques Marsal and their dog were hiking in the countryside outside the village of Montignac, in the heart of the lush and rustic Dordogne, in what was then wartime Vichy France. The dog, happy to be free, ran among the rocks and the bushes that dotted the steep hill they were climbing. But when the boys reached the top, they realized that the dog was no longer with them. It was dusk, and they began to retrace their steps in search of the animal.

About a hundred yards down the hill, they suddenly heard muffled barks and whimpers. They approached what seemed to be the source of the barking and realized that their dog had fallen into the mouth of a cave obscured by some bushes. Using their flashlights, they helped each other down into a deep cave, where they finally found the dog. Delighted by this surprising discovery, the boys and their dog continued into the cave, where they found a dreamlike display of prehistoric art that made this cave, which was later named Lascaux, world famous.

Ravidat and Marsal told their old schoolmaster, Léon Laval, about their amazing discovery, and he immediately tried to notify the most famous prehistorian in France about the new cave—Laval wrote to Abbé Henri Breuil.

But in September 1940, Breuil was in Brive, after having visited several other caves in the Dordogne. He did not get Laval's letter, but a childhood friend, Maurice Thaon, came to visit him in Brive and showed Breuil sketches he had made two days earlier of paintings found in this newly discovered cave. Breuil quickly left for the town of Terrasson. There, a local doctor drove him to the hill above Montignac, where the entrance of the cave of Lascaux was located. Breuil marveled at the paintings in this cave—they were more resplendent than any he had ever seen, and when he departed, he vowed to return soon. He described what had happened to his friend Broderick:

> After having informed the Prefect of the Dordogne, the Director of Prehistoric Antiquities of the province, M. Peyrony, and the owners of the site, the Comte and Comtesse Emanuel de La Rochefoucauld, I was again at Lascaux, with them, on September 27 and 28. Then, on October 14, I took up my quarters at the country house of M. de Montardy, quite near the cave in which I spent most of every day. . . . [The cave entrance] gave onto a steep slope, slippery and slimy, under the limestone covering the floor of the cavern was a reddish, semi-liquid mass of clay, with flakes of worked flint of poor quality, but Paleolithic, some fragments of reindeer

horns and many pieces of conifer charcoal—the
remains of the grotto's lighting system.[1]

Lascaux, like many decorated caves, has a complex of galleries, and by the time Breuil had arrived at the scene, only the
easiest ones to enter had been explored. In order to reach deeper
into this cavern, Breuil set to work and dredged up the bottom
of the cave, removing debris. Material that had been suspended
inside the cave's natural chimney collapsed, opening up the area
and allowing passage into the cave. There was much water on
the ground, and although Breuil and his colleagues tried to walk
on an axial passage leading farther down into a location now
called the pit (or shaft; in French, *puits*)—an enigmatic place to
which we will soon return—the mud and the loose earth gave
way under their feet, and they had to abandon that effort.

The place now called the Nave, an important location of
paintings, was also impenetrable, and the group had to cease
exploration for the day and wait for better conditions when the
ground would settle after drying a bit. When they returned several days later, they were able to enter into the depths of this
mysterious cave. Lascaux has amazing paintings and engravings.
The paintings are in color, as in Font-de-Gaume and Altamira,
and they feature a rich display of superimposed animals: bison,
horses, aurochs, and other animals that are common to the art
of the Dordogne.

Breuil authenticated the cave's drawings and certified them
as Magdalenian, dated to 15,000 to 13,000 years ago. Within a
few months, once the Abbé's work on this cave came to public
attention, Lascaux became a household name. This brought the
artistic work of our ancestors to the forefront of public interest.
Until 1963, when serious damage to the art in this cave from
human presence became evident and the cave was closed to the
public, Lascaux was visited by twelve hundred people every day.

Breuil had injured his eye badly several months earlier, and the pain made it impossible for him to copy the art of Lascaux. Others did it instead. Breuil did, however, conduct the analysis and authentication of the paintings.

The art of Lascaux has since been dated with radiocarbon, and the dates were found to be 15,516 years before the present, with a margin of error of several hundred years. This dating places the artists of Lascaux well inside the Magdalenian period.[2]

Breuil was not only an indefatigable explorer and investigator of cave art—he was, above all, a thinking man. Everything he saw and explored made him think and theorize. He marveled at the incredible paintings he found in prehistoric caves and asked the question Why? Breuil answered this question in a thoughtful way, theorizing that the Magdalenian artists and those of earlier Cro-Magnon cultures were concerned with hunting, because they depended on it for their survival. They drew images of beautiful animals as a way of praying to their God or gods to supply them with animals. But the Abbé could also see in these drawings, paintings, and engravings an art for its own sake.

Breuil has been criticized by later scholars who hold opposing views, foremost among them the French prehistorian Jean Clottes. Clottes, whose work has recently received much attention in France, conducted much field work in Paleolithic caves. We will shortly discuss Clottes's own hypotheses about the purpose of cave art.

• • •

In analyzing prehistoric cave art, perhaps the most important thing to understand is that every decorated cave is a cohesive unit. Today we know that it would be grossly misleading to examine each work of art in a cave as a separate entity. Rather, the entire collection of paintings, drawings, and engravings must not only be seen as a logical ensemble, but must also be considered within the topographical context of the natural cave environment itself.

There is ample evidence within the caves that the prehistoric artists had intended each entire cave to be taken as a unit. First, the texture of the cave walls is often used in making the art. The Cro-Magnon artists took time and effort to find cave wall surfaces of certain shapes to give their creations particular three-dimensional qualities. In addition, the animal depictions on cave walls or ceilings are always arranged with much forethought—they are never randomly placed. If a bull is depicted opposite a horse, there is a reason for this placement, as evidenced by the fact that such spatial connections repeat themselves from cave to cave.

There are also very important progressions within caves: the art starts with certain kinds of animals and changes and intensifies in density, color, and the aspect and demeanor of the depicted animals as one goes farther inside the cave. Lascaux is perhaps the best example of these connections and relationships among the animals and between the terrain and the images.

The diverticulum (the Axial Gallery) of Lascaux is a place of artworks that are drawn, painted, and engraved. All three kinds of art are shown in this main passageway into the cave. The quality of execution of this multi-type art is exceptional, and this is what has led to Lascaux becoming the most famous decorated cave in the world.

The cave of Lascaux is generally divided into seven key sections. They are

1. The Rotunda (the Hall of the Bulls)
2. The Axial Gallery (diverticulum)
3. The Passage
4. The Apse

5. The Pit (or shaft)

6. The Nave (the Long Gallery)

7. The Chamber of Felines

The entrance to the cave leads directly to the Rotunda (Hall of the Bulls, "La Salle des Taureaux"). This collection of depictions of aurochs accompanied by other animals ends in a narrowing of the cave walls about fifty feet farther on, which makes continuing in this direction impossible. This gallery is imposing: the bulls are huge—seventeen feet high, as compared to the ones in Altamira, which measure a maximum height of only seven feet. But in another direction, the Rotunda gives way to a corridor that bifurcates in two directions: one to the Pit, on the right, and the other, on the left, leads to the Nave (also called the Long Gallery). A full hundred yards after the Rotunda, the Nave ends in the Chamber of Felines: a medium-size hall with pictures of lions, accompanied by other animals.

The Axial Gallery, by its very location within the cave, forms a natural continuation with the same painted figures as those found in the Rotunda. The artists have clearly emphasized this apparent continuity by using the same elements in both locations—but with a subtle dynamic change. There are far fewer engravings in the Axial Gallery than there are in the Rotunda and in other parts of Lascaux. The painted animals in the Rotunda appear to march together right into the Axial Gallery. And the same subjects are taken up in the two locations in a natural way. Thus, one comes to the inescapable conclusion that there is a unity of themes and actors in this large drama.

The separation between the two walls of the Axial Gallery varies from about five to fifteen feet throughout the length of this natural hallway. One can look at the art either across the hall at two opposing panels as one progresses through this part of the cave or, alternatively, by staying on one side only without looking across. The painted subjects here follow a uniform structure either way. The best description of the art here is that a large animal is always in the center of each composition on a panel, and the central figure is surrounded by smaller animals.

In terms of the main animals, the depictions along the north face of this part of the cave have been titled as follows: *The Cow with the Black Head*, *The Great Bull*, and *The Falling Horse*. The opposing face of this part of the cave, and the ceiling, can be described by focusing on the main animal of each location: *The Affronted Ibexes*, *The Jumping Cow*, and *The "Chinese Horses"* (so named because they resemble horses in ancient Chinese paintings).[3] The animals here are horses, aurochs (wild bulls and cows), deer, ibex, and a bison. There is also a great abundance of signs here— of both categories defined by Leroi-Gourhan: narrow signs and wide ones. Plate 5 is the Great Bull with horses of the cave of Lascaux.

Plate 5. The Great Bull with horses of the cave of Lascaux.

In four of the seven main concentrations of art in the Lascaux cave, the bovines—aurochs and bison—are the main animals depicted. They are accompanied by horses, which form their own group, in turn flanked by either ibex or deer. The bovines are by far the largest figures shown on the walls of the main part of Lascaux, even as compared to the horses, and their presence seems to form the primary theme.

Elsewhere in the cave, the horses dominate in number, although they are smaller and more discreetly represented. But there is one exception to the small size of the horses: *The Great Bull* of Lascaux, surrounded by small animals, stands next to a big horse. There are many signs surrounding, and sometimes placed on top of, the animals in this part of the cave. These belong to both the narrow and the wide categories of signs identified by Leroi-Gourhan.

The animals here seem to follow some mysterious mythology. Their compositions and their positions on the walls attest to it: the kinds of animals seem to be dictated by certain laws, and their movements are fanciful: jumping cows, falling horses, leaping ibex.

In addition, there are "imaginary" animals as well: the strange Licorne (literally, "unicorn," but here with two horns) of Lascaux—an animal that looks like a large aurochs but has two very long, straight horns that stretch far in front of it. Animals considered imaginary are also found in other caves, such as the so-called "antelopes" of Pech Merle, which are not antelopes but rather creatures with small heads and long necks and bodies that resemble those of horses. Scholars have assumed that such animals never existed and that the Paleolithic artists simply imagined them. But we can't be sure about this hypothesis. The reason scientists think so is that unlike mammoths and other animals that once existed and are no more, we have never found any bone fossils belonging to an animal like the Licorne of Lascaux or the "antelopes" of Pech Merle. But the absence of fossils is far from proof of anything. We don't have enough fossils, and they do not belong to skeletons of a complete animal in any one excavation for us to make a definitive determination. In 2008, a deer was born in a game reserve near Prato, Italy, with one horn in the center of its forehead.[4] All that the cave artists would have needed was to have observed one such animal, perhaps born of a genetic defect, for their subjects to have been perfectly real and not at all imaginary. Our labeling them as such is a reflection of our scientific hubris. Why would we even assume that we could have found the fossils of all living things that ever inhabited the planet?

In Lascaux, the "imaginary unicorn" somehow exists in perfect harmony within the rest of the animals on the walls; it doesn't seem odd or mythical. This is not to say that the cave artists didn't celebrate their new ability to think creatively by drawing fantasized creatures. Perhaps that's what they did. But the rarity of such depictions and the great naturalistic detail with which they drew all other animals makes me think that they stuck to real subjects. Perhaps they valued rare animals whenever they found them in nature—abnormalities or very rare species—and drew them for that reason. If inventiveness had been the artists' motive, I would have expected them to draw many more imaginary animals.

• • •

The signs in Lascaux are physically associated with the various animals in some systematic way and seem to have been placed there for specific reasons, which are unknown to us.

André Leroi-Gourhan and Annette Laming-Emperaire have constructed their theories about cave art and signs based on the complete collection found at Lascaux, with its apparent unity of composition. It was clear to them, once they inspected Lascaux in the early 1960s, that there had to be strong connections that made Lascaux a single artistic unit, pregnant with meanings. They then set out to understand the significance of this artwork and used the art found in other caves to further develop their theory and to test it with new information. The result was the most comprehensive, scientifically supported, and logically based theory ever put forward about the art and the signs of decorated prehistoric caves.

11

The Enigma of the Pit

THE PIT OF LASCAUX IS LOCATED AT A DEPTH OF ABOUT twenty feet below the normal ground surface of the cave and is accessible through a narrow hole in the cave floor. A ladder has been placed there, for use by researchers, but visitors—while the cave was still open to the public—were never allowed into the pit. Presumably, the Magdalenians who had worked here used their own makeshift ladder, allowing them access to this difficult-to-reach location.

In general, the art found inside decorated caves in Europe does not present a narrative, something that is obviously a story. Animals are overlaid on one another, without terrain and with few humanlike figures. But inside the Pit of Lascaux—the deepest and most central, yet most hidden and inaccessible, location in the entire cave—there is a composite drawing that could not be interpreted as anything but a story: either real or imaginary, and perhaps mythical or allegorical. The scene drawn inside the Pit at Lascaux is perhaps the most enigmatic of all prehistoric images.

In the center of the scene is a bison, believed by some to be female. The bison's stomach is pierced by a spear, and the entrails are exposed and touching the ground. The bison's head is turned backward in what is obviously great pain, looking at the injured back of its body. A lance lies on the ground nearby. Next to it lies a man, face up with spread arms. His fingers are birdlike (there are four of them), and his face is that of a bird. Next to him, on a pole stuck in the ground, is a bird whose face resembles that of the man. The man is ithyphallic. Off to the left side, a rhinoceros is walking away from the scene, tail raised; there is a series of dots under the tail. No one knows what this strange scene means, although several theories have been proposed about it. Plate 6 shows the scene from the Pit at Lascaux.

Plate 6. The scene of the Pit at Lascaux.

Abbé Henri Breuil considered the possibility that the pit may have been the burial ground of the man, the "birdman" felled by a bison while trying to hunt it. But this theory was proved wrong. Breuil himself dug under the pit and found no human remains or even animal bones. And no signs of human burial have ever been found anywhere in Lascaux.

The meaning of the composition in the Pit of Lascaux has continued to puzzle scholars for decades. Recently, a Belgian professor named Jacques Picard published a book devoted to his theory about this scene, called *Le mythe fondateur de Lascaux* (The founding myth of Lascaux), in which he argued that the depiction here is of a symbolic myth about early human morality. Clearly, there is a story told here, which is different in its form from the art of all other caves, and in fact different from the rest of the magnificent art at Lascaux.

According to Picard, the gravely wounded bison is female and represents the mother; the ithyphallic birdman is her son, and he is also dying. Both are put to death because of the crime of incest. The rhinoceros walking away from the scene is the disgusted father. The bird imagery—the fact that the man has birdlike characteristics, and there is a bird on a pole nearby (any bird image is very rare in Paleolithic art)—was not explained by Picard.[1]

It is difficult to say whether there is any convincing evidence for such an interpretation; there is certainly no way of proving or disproving such a theory. All that we have are the actual images from the cave. Although the bison may represent a female, the ithyphallic man lying supine on the ground may simply be a male symbol. The fact that the bison is wounded is rare: we know that wounded animals appear infrequently in prehistoric cave art. Perhaps the scene could equally be interpreted as a moral law against bestiality or any number of other possibilities. Male and female symbols, as we will see, are the basis of Leroi-Gourhan's theories. But the symbolism in this story remains a mystery.

When the art of Lascaux was first published in 1949, the photographs of the scene of the pit were retouched so that the erection of the birdman would not show. At that time, people were sensitive to sexual imagery in all art, including any symbolic prehistorical images.

But Picard was far from the first to be intrigued by the bizarre scene of the Pit of Lascaux and to offer his interpretation. The French philosopher Georges Bataille spent many years on this topic, and many of his books, articles, and lectures attempt to address the disturbing mystery of the images in the Pit of Lascaux. In his book devoted to the intellectual interpretation of the idea of eroticism (*L'Éroticisme* [Paris: Minuit, 1957]), Bataille uses the scene from the Pit at Lascaux to argue that eroticism is linked in the human mind with sacrifice, anguish, and ecstasy.

In Bataille's view, the scene from Lascaux involves the sacrifice of the bison. He sees the birdman as a shaman who has entered a state of ecstasy brought on by the fear of the wild animal and excitement by its subsequent demise. This state has induced sexual arousal.[2]

In the posthumous edited collection of some of Bataille's lectures, *The Cradle of Humanity: Prehistoric Art and Culture* (New York: Zone, 2005), one sees how the philosopher further pursued this idea. The editor's introduction, written by Stuart Kendall, says that in Bataille's interpretation, the man in the pit identifies with the dying animal.

> In the scene of the pit, this impossible identifica-
> tion appears in the form of an impossible figu-
> ration, an image of the impossible: a disfigured
> bird-man falling, sex erect, beside a beautifully
> rendered bison, respected in attentive realism
> but dying, the life inside him pouring forth from
> his belly. Images of cruelty are cruel images: they
> ask us to identify with our own annihilation. This
> impossible recognition remains the key to the eth-
> ics proposed by Bataille. We cannot steel ourselves
> to horror; we cannot hope to endure. Nor can we
> hope to share the burden of the pain of others.[3]

And in a major essay in this collection, titled "A Visit to Lascaux," Bataille said,

> Let's take a closer look at the only clear repre-
> sentation of a man found in the Lascaux cave [in
> the scene in the pit]. You see that it is crudely
> schematic. It appeals to our intellect, not our
> senses. It is an intelligible sign. I don't mean that
> it entails a kind of writing, but moving from the
> image to writing, we would only have to multiply

the signs; we would also have to simplify them and render them conventionally systematic, yet it is clearly a question, for figurative art, of a completely different direction, of another open path.[4]

Thus, Bataille sees the scene in the Pit at Lascaux—more than the signs that appear everywhere in Paleolithic caves—as a kind of early pictorial writing. Here we have an actual story, which he tries to imagine further by dissecting what happens in a hunt: there is fear, excitement, and also a compassion for the animal being hunted.

This is one interpretation of the scene of the pit, but it leaves out whatever meaning there may be in the image of the retreating rhinoceros (which some scholars believe is the cause of the disembowelment of the bison, because, they think, this injury could not have been caused by the spear). It also does not explain the bird on the pole or why the man has birdlike features. And it is perhaps a stretch to assume that the man's erection was caused by the excitement of the hunt. The scene of the Pit in Lascaux thus remains one of the greatest unsolved mysteries in Paleolithic "pictorial story telling."

• • •

A variety of styles and theories among researchers address the deep mystery of the meaning of Paleolithic cave art. Much attention has focused on the Pit of Lascaux because its artwork is so puzzling. But even elsewhere in European caves, the enigma is palpable.

Breuil was an indefatigable pioneer who rushed to every new cave and quickly established himself as a world authority on the meaning of this art. Scientific methods were not widely available when he started, so Breuil made up the science as he went along. (The fairly accurate radiocarbon dating system, which uses the rate of decay of radioactive carbon in a comparison of its concentration in ancient artifacts with that of the environment and extrapolates a date estimate, was available only from the late 1940s onward.)

Breuil's thinking was rooted in the idea that Paleolithic man was a hunter and his interest in animals was driven, first and foremost, by the needs of the hunt. To this assumption, Breuil imputed some vague idea of a "religion," which came in part from his training as a priest. But it stopped there. He did not pursue the concept of an ancient religion whose purpose was to worship a god or a deity in supplication for a successful hunt. Even though he was technically a priest, Breuil had little real interest in pursuing religion as a career and was excited to follow his passion of rushing from cave to cave, establishing himself as an expert and inventing a new science—all the while supported by the deep pockets of Prince Albert of Monaco.

Jean Clottes, on the other hand, took Breuil's hypotheses and criticized some of them but overall pursued the idea of the hunt to a kind of conclusion. The religion aspect that Clottes attributed to the Stone Age artists was clad in the guise of shamanism. And while Breuil was the peripatetic discoverer and copier of cave drawings and paintings, ever on the move, Clottes is the methodical tabulator: he is a keeper of lists. His theory is a particular twist on Breuil's deeper results, and it is somewhat limited in scope. We will now meet a young woman who had greater vision in her approach to this persistent mystery.

12

The Groundbreaking Work of Annette Laming-Emperaire

WHEN ABBÉ HENRI BREUIL ANALYZED THE FINDINGS in Lascaux in 1940, he concluded that the bison (or wild ox) was the dominant animal, and it was accompanied by signs that resembled arrows. Breuil paid considerable attention to the other signs as well: rows of dots, lines, and other geometrical designs. The wide "tectiform" signs he interpreted as perhaps representing traps, because he was convinced that success in the hunt was a key reason that prehistoric man had created the art of the caves. If arrowheads represented a desire for hunting prey animals, then the wider sign could be interpreted as a desire to trap them. Such a sign is shown below.

In addition to these hypotheses, there were related ones. There was a notion of "sympathetic magic"—depicting wounded animals as part of a shamanistic ritual aimed at capturing them. And there was the idea that drawings of composite human-animal figures found in a few caves (although rare) represented "sorcerers." These theories remained as plausible explanations of the meaning of cave art for some time. But then a young woman with great talent entered the field of prehistoric cave art analysis. She would change the way we think about Paleolithic cave art.

• • •

Annette Laming-Emperaire (1917–1977) was born in Petrograd, Russia, and came to France to study prehistory at the Sorbonne. When she was a graduate student in Paris, World War II interrupted her career. She left her studies to join the French Resistance, where she distinguished herself with great courage. At war's end in 1945, when she resumed her research, she turned her attention to the prehistory of South America. She studied artifacts from that continent and later would work for some time in the field in Tierra del Fuego, at the tip of the South American continent, analyzing remains of early human habitation dating to about 12,000 years ago.

In Paris, Laming-Emperaire came in contact with Breuil, who had recently analyzed the art of Lascaux, and she was intrigued. She was greatly influenced by the Abbé's work and initiated her own study of the paintings, drawings, engravings, and signs found in this important cave. Her work resulted in a number of seminal books on Lascaux and other prehistoric cave art. She decided to switch her doctoral thesis topic from something related to South American prehistory to a new analysis of European cave art.

Laming-Emperaire brought to this realm a refreshingly new approach that freed the study of prehistoric cave art from the strong influence of Breuil and other schools of thought, which advocated the idea of shamanism. Pursuing her dissertation research at the Sorbonne, Laming-Emperaire started to work with Professor André Leroi-Gourhan (1911–1986).

Like Laming-Emperaire, Leroi-Gourhan had also served in the French Resistance during the war. In 1944, he was assigned the enviable task of reclaiming for France the art treasures of the Louvre, which had been looted by the Nazis and had later been retaken by Allied Forces and held at the Chateau de Valençay. Leroi-Gourhan catalogued these invaluable treasures and supervised their return to Paris.

He had made a career as an expert on the archaeology of the South Pacific, but when Laming-Emperaire approached him to request him to supervise her thesis on European cave art, he was fascinated by her new ideas about the interpretation of the paintings and the signs. Not only did he agree to work with her, but he also changed his own research direction in response to this new interest and would eventually take Laming-Emperaire's results and expand on them considerably. Ultimately, even though he would do important work in evolution, philosophy, and anthropology, his greatest legacy would be the progress he made on the topic Laming-Emperaire had steered him to. Laming-Emperaire, intrigued not only by the animals of Lascaux and elsewhere, but, equally important, by the mysterious signs that abound in caves, would become the first scholar to seriously study the symbolism of Lascaux and other Paleolithic caves in France and Spain.

Laming-Emperaire began to address the mystery of the purpose and meaning of cave art by rejecting the "ethnographic" approach, as she called it. That is, she resolved to focus on the archaeological findings of cave art on their own, without imposing any preconceived ideas about who created these elements and why, in a way that would reflect a modern observer's inherent biases. When looking at a prehistoric decorated cave, the modern observer must not apply to it any prior knowledge about present-day "primitive" art or the customs of existing societies.

Laming-Emperaire believed that this approach ensured the objectivity of the modern observer. In a sense, a visit to a prehistoric cave is a kind of time travel to the distant past, tens of thousands of years ago, and to the beginnings of human artistic creativity. We must therefore view the art exactly as it is—no more and no less.

With this strategy as her guide, Laming-Emperaire first realized that each cave containing European cave art must be taken as a whole. It is not constructive to consider separate drawings, paintings, or engravings on cave walls. Rather, one must look at the entire cave in context. Terrain is never part of the context regarding the animals and signs depicted on cave walls: there are no trees, rivers, or mountains, and the humanlike figures are always ambiguous, imprecisely drawn, and rare. But according to Laming-Emperaire's view, the context of each painting in each cave is the totality of all of the other works of art in that cave—and of the cave's topography itself.

She also noted a very important distinction that she recognized among various kinds of prehistoric art. According to Laming-Emperaire, there is a noticeable difference between the art covering the walls of open rock shelters in France and elsewhere, as well as the mobile art found everywhere in Europe, and the art displayed in deep decorated caves such as Lascaux, Niaux, Pech Merle, Font-de-Gaume, Rouffignac, and others.

The art that appears above the surface of the earth, on rocks or on decorated items, depicts few animals, and they tend to be diminutive and unimposing ones: usually deer or reindeer and a few other small animals. In the deep sanctuaries of decorated caves, however, one finds a much greater density and variety of animals: bison, horses, mammoths, lions, rhinoceroses, and so on. Here, too, we find many signs, and the animals themselves are more imposing than those depicted outside the deep caverns; they also include, on rare occasions, mythical animals such as the Licorne of Lascaux.[1]

Laming-Emperaire hypothesized that the people who depicted the animals on the walls of the deep halls of caves felt small and unimportant as compared with the animals. To support this idea, she pointed out that the human figures are rarely found in caves, and they are only schematically drawn—they are never portrayed in precise detail, as are the animals. She also claimed that these human figures are often shown as pierced by arrows and are small in stature.

Laming-Emperaire also argued that the few figures that are interpreted as half-human and half-animal, often dubbed "sorcerers," which may represent people in animal guise or masks, are not sorcerers or shamans but rather humans who felt small and unimportant and therefore disguised themselves as animals to seem more significant.

But, according to Laming-Emperaire, it is the relationship among the animals that is paramount in the art of the caves. And here is where she made her greatest contribution to the study of prehistoric cave art. By noticing that if we look at each cave in its own totality, as a uniform whole, then one thing stands out very obviously: it is the clear pattern of pairing a horse with a bison or a horse with an aurochs.

She also pointed out alternative pairings of animals found in cave art: a mammoth with an ibex, a bison and a boar, or a lion with a horse. These pairings—and especially the most common horse-bison or horse-aurochs couples—repeat themselves again and again in prehistoric caves that date across many millennia. Laming-Emperaire stressed that such a persistent phenomenon must be significant. There has to be a reason Paleolithic people depicted these pairs of animals. This pattern could not have arisen purely by chance, certainly not when repeated over thousands of years and over a wide geographical area. She noted, however, that the meaning of these pairings was yet unclear: it could be mythical, an oral history of a group of people and their relationships to certain animals; it could be a religious depiction of some significance; or it could be an ancient metaphysical concept.

Laming-Emperaire then proposed a key idea that would later be pursued much further by Leroi-Gourhan. Among the possible reasons for the curious pairings of animals of particular kinds, she wrote, "[These relations] could concretize a very ancient metaphysical system of the world, in which each species, animal or human, plays a part, and in which the sexual division of the beings plays a primordial role."[2]

Laming-Emperaire next addressed the mystery of the signs, but here her analysis simply considered the reigning theories of the time, which held—through the work of Breuil and others—that the signs have to do with the hunt. Some are arrows, some are traps, and others may be signatures of the artists or other identifying symbols of tribes or groups or individuals. Again, it was Leroi-Gourhan who took the analysis to a much higher level. He seized on Laming-Emperaire's idea that the couplings of the animals themselves in cave art may bear some symbolic sexual division, and he interpreted all of the signs found in prehistoric caves as strictly sexual in their symbolism.

Laming-Emperaire concluded her analysis of the meaning of cave art, in her published dissertation, as follows:

At the end of this study, we are more than ever conscious of the uncertainties and the lacunae, of the necessity of taking it up and completing it, and of the impossibility of considering only single elements of analysis and reconstituting the extraordinary universe of the people of the Paleolithic as inscribed on the walls of caves and rock shelters. It allows us, however, to pass from the notion of a magical Paleolithic art to that of an art that is far more complex and rich, pregnant with a new significance. We see in the lines of this art an unexpected world, a mythical world that was already rich in traditions, which were undoubtedly preceded by other, earlier traditions, now lost forever. For the first time in the history of humanity, the artists of quaternary caves fixed on rock their representations of humans and Earth, their quest to integrate themselves into the great animal adventure that played out around their encampments. It is well worth the effort to try to decipher this first Treatise of Nature.[3]

Laming-Emperaire began working on her doctoral dissertation in 1948, but because of a serious accident, which kept her unable to publish for some time, followed by a fire that destroyed an earlier version of her manuscript, and her frequent research trips to South America over the intervening years, her thesis was published only in 1962.

By then, her colleague in prehistoric cave research and former professor, André Leroi-Gourhan, was well on his way with his own extensions of her theory. He was only six years her senior, but his career overtook hers by leaps and bounds, and he was able to formulate groundbreaking conclusions, many of which were founded on Laming-Emperaire's early observations of the cohesive, uniform nature of prehistoric cave art.

Despite the setbacks, Laming-Emperaire enjoyed a fruitful career in prehistory in France and traveled abroad frequently, spending months and years at many important and yet-unexplored archaeological sites in South America. In 1977, in Brazil, Annette Laming-Emperaire died tragically from a leak in a gas heater.

13

Prehistoric Objets d'Art

IN EUROPE, OBJECTS BEARING ARTISTIC ENGRAVINGS OR otherwise shaped in esthetic ways turned up several decades before the "official" birth of prehistory with the first discoveries of cave art. In 1834, a French explorer named A. Brouillet found a bone with two incised images of deer inside the cave of La Chaffaud, in the French department of Vienne. Scholars who inspected this unusual find attributed it to the work of "Celts"— the name given in those days to all inhabitants of France who supposedly lived there before the Roman conquest of Gaul.

For reasons of religion and tradition, no one at that time seriously suspected that people had lived in Europe tens of thousands of years ago. Christian belief in the genealogy of humanity, implied by the stories in Genesis, forbade any assumptions that people had existed much earlier than 6,000 years ago. There have been many biblically based calculations, the most commonly quoted one by the Anglican archbishop of Armagh, James Ussher, who claimed that the world was created on

October 23 in 4004 BC. Christians could not imagine Europe being inhabited by human cultures 30,000 years ago.

Other art objects were found, yet were not determined to be prehistorical, in the modern sense of the word, but rather Celtic. Then around 1870, some bones bearing engraved images of mammoths, bison, and lions—animals that clearly no longer existed, at least not in Europe—were discovered at Mascat, near Lourdes in the Pyrenees, and at the famous site of La Madeleine.

These findings made it obvious that the people who had created this mobile art (as distinguished from the stationary art on cave walls, to be discovered later) had to have coexisted with the extinct animals they portrayed. This deduction forced scholars to reexamine the Celtic hypothesis, and, slowly, people came to the understanding that humans had lived in Europe much earlier than was previously assumed.

After the discoveries of cave art, archaeologists continued to unearth extensive evidence of Cro-Magnon life, including the remains of hearths, bones of animals that had been consumed by these people, and mobile art. An interesting finding was emerging: not far from every decorated cave, such as Rouffignac, Lascaux, or Niaux, there was a dwelling cave.

The Cro-Magnons never lived in their decorated caves, and in fact, they visited these caves only rarely (as inferred from footsteps found in caves and an almost complete lack of remains of meals or stone tools). They lived in nearby shallow caves or rock shelters—places that enjoyed at least some sunlight. In these open caves or shelters, they left evidence of their occupation. The cave of La Vache, for example, lies across a valley from Niaux in the Pyrenees, and it was here that the artists who decorated Niaux are believed to have lived. Bone remains of the meals eaten by these people revealed what they consumed: mostly reindeer meat, some ibex, and fish.

Perhaps not surprisingly (since this is a mountainous region and not a prairie or a plain), no bison bones were ever discovered at the cave of La Vache. The hunter-gatherers of La Vache, including the artists who decorated Niaux, hunted no bison. So why is the bison the dominant animal in the art of Niaux? Henri Breuil did not answer this question. But others have suggested that the people of La Vache-Niaux were nomads who had come there from the plains to the north and painted the animals they hoped to hunt once they returned to the region where the bison roamed. But then other problems with this interpretation arose.

The cave of Niaux includes drawings of large felines, and other caves show rhinoceroses and bears. From an analysis of all of the remains of ancient Cro-Magnon hearths, it became clear that these people did not eat large animals such as lions, rhinos, and bears. So why were these animals painted, if success in the hunt was the purpose of the cave art? In addition, archaeology has revealed that, by far, the animal most commonly eaten by the Cro-Magnons was not the bison—it was the reindeer. During the Ice Age, reindeer herds were very numerous, and the animal was easily hunted. Most of the bones found in Cro-Magnon sites were those of reindeer. But the reindeer itself very rarely appears in cave art. Something was very wrong with the theory.

The mystery grew further. Breuil had never attempted to explain the myriad sexual symbols in the caves: drawings of vulvas, stylized or realistic, as well as schematic sketches of ithyphallic men. And then came other unexplained elements. Along with bones, stone tools, and the remains of ancient hearths, archaeologists found many ancient objets d'art.

These were handles for stone tools, made of mammoth ivory or reindeer horn, as well as statuettes. The statuettes were of naked women (they are often called "Venus statuettes"), and the handles of implements were often in the form of a penis. These objects were unearthed in great abundance in Cro-Magnon dwelling places—most notably, Magdalenian—in vast areas of Europe. But Breuil ignored them. Some people think that because of his religion, Breuil could not address issues of sex. But this assumption doesn't seem to hold much sway.

André Leroi-Gourhan discovered an interesting property of the Venus statuettes and other full-body human female representations in Paleolithic art. He noted that all of them tend to be shaped like a diamond—thin at the top and the bottom, and thick in the middle.

The "Stone Age Venuses," as they have been called, attracted much attention when the first one was found in 1896. In fact, the discoverer of the first such statuette named it Venus as a kind of joke, since the statuette was of an overweight woman— by today's standards, at least. It had exaggerated breasts and pelvic region and heavy thighs and belly. The first ones were even called "Steatopygous Venuses," or "Fat Venuses." The breasts, the abdomen, and the pelvic region are placed within an approximate circle, and the entire body is in the shape of a diamond.

Plate 7. The *Venus of Willendorf.*

The most famous one of all is the *Venus of Willendorf,* discovered by Josef Szombathy in Austria in 1903—years after the first discoveries of such statuettes in the 1800s. This statuette captured our imagination because of its detailed features, and it has worked itself into the human consciousness. It is shown in Plate 7.

These statuettes are sometimes called the "Aurignacian women," on the supposition that they are generally around 30,000 years old, thus Aurignacian. Recent studies, however, have placed many of them in the later Solutrean period.

According to Leroi-Gourhan, "To assume that actual Aurignacian women were overweight, based on the appearance
of the statuettes, would be similar to deducing the physiology of
the modern French woman based on the works of Picasso."[1]

It is also worth noting a strange dichotomy. Europe at the
time of the Aurignacians and later Paleolithic peoples was a very
cold continent: this period was within the cycles of the Ice Age.
During this era, women, as well as men, were always clothed very
warmly in order to survive. And yet, with very few exceptions—
and some of them ambiguous—the women of the Paleolithic are
always depicted nude. The question is why.

It is important to understand both the similarities and the
contrasts between images created in deep caves and those found
on the earth's surface: on rock faces in the open or as portable art
objects. Among the mobile art objects, depictions of the penis
are common and far outnumber any representations of vulvas.
Inside deep caves, there are very few portrayals of penises; one
such case is in the cave of Bara Bahau in the Dordogne. While at
the same time, images of vulvas are numerous in deep caves.

Portrayals of naked women are common outside of caves,
both on rock art in France and as Venus statuettes found all over
Europe. This artwork shows the woman's full body or most of
it. In deep caves, however, the female depictions either portray
the vulva alone or are schematic drawings of all or part of the
body. In addition, although human images in caves are mere
sketches—some of them only barely recognizable as human—
there are very detailed depictions of human beings in the art
found outside the caves. On a rock in La Marche in France
there are more than a hundred portraits of men and women;
some of them look very similar to modern-day cartoons.[2]

Another rock discovered at the same location has engraved
images of two men who look as if they are involved in a fight.
These images are all clear—they show faces, and sometimes

bodies—and are thus very different from the mysterious, schematic, and ambiguous rare "humanoid" images found in deep caves. It is obvious that Paleolithic artists avoided making human depictions in cave art as much as possible. Was this perhaps a manifestation of a religious rule?

Women's images outside deep caves took other forms as well. Figurines of women's heads, showing facial features and finely coiffed hair, have turned up in geographically faraway places throughout the European continent. Among these are the well-known statuettes found in Dolni Vestonice in the Czech Republic and the sculpture of a feminine head at Brassempouy. Others have been unearthed in Italy, Austria, and Russia.

In Laussel, in France, an engraving of a naked woman was discovered on a very large limestone rock that acted as part of a natural wall protecting a Gravettian habitation in the Dordogne. The woman is holding a horn, thus the engraving was dubbed *The Venus with the Horn*. The rock with the engraving has been removed from this location, and it can now be seen at the Museum of Aquitaine in Bordeaux.

Many similar rock engravings have been found in France, geographically dispersed over sizable areas of the country. What is the meaning of these images?

One thing we do know is that there seems to be a significant difference between the mobile and rock art found all over Europe and the artwork located in deep caves in France and Spain. Both forms of art include animal images, but the types of animals are different: small and tame creatures on mobile art; larger, more significant animals, generally depicted in more detail, on cave walls. Regarding artwork that shows humans, the opposite is true. Whether in caves or outside, representations of human figures are often sexual in nature, but they are portrayed realistically and in more detail in artwork that is found outside, both mobile and on rock faces. In the rare instances that human images appear inside caves, they are usually reduced to sexual organs.

This leads us to conclude that outside art, on rock faces or as statuettes, served a very different purpose from the artwork created in deep caves. Perhaps deep caverns were considered places of religious worship, or maybe another tradition dictated that human figures cannot be detailed and that animals must dominate in the depths of the caverns.

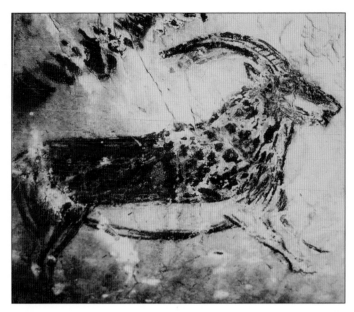

Plate 1. Drawing of a Pyrenean ibex from the wall of the Black Salon, cave of Niaux, Magdalenian period, around 14,000 years ago.

Plate 2. A Mousterian stone ax.

Plate 3. Mammoth and ibex on the Grand Ceiling of the cave of Rouffignac.

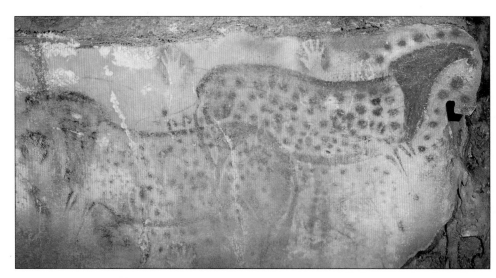

Plate 4. The dotted horses of the cave of Pech Merle.

Plate 5. The Great Bull with horses of the cave of Lascaux.

Plate 6. The scene of the Pit at Lascaux.

Plate 7.
The *Venus of Willendorf*.

Plate 8.
The *White Lady* of Africa.

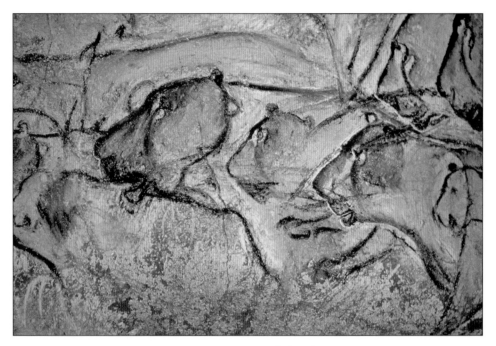

Plate 9. The hunting lions of the Chauvet cave.

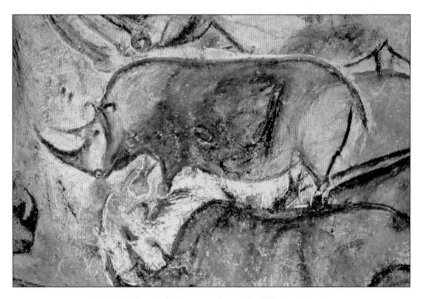

Plate 10. A rhinoceros from the Chauvet cave.

Plate 11. The *Panel of the Horses*, with a rhinoceros below, Chauvet cave.

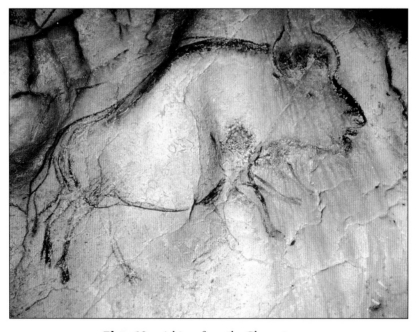

Plate 12. A bison from the Chauvet cave.

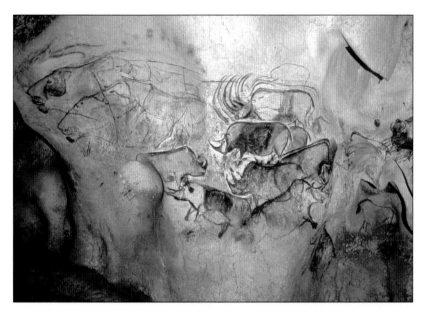

Plate 13. The Big Lions (left) and the *Panel of the Rhinoceroses* on the left wall of the End Chamber, Chauvet cave.

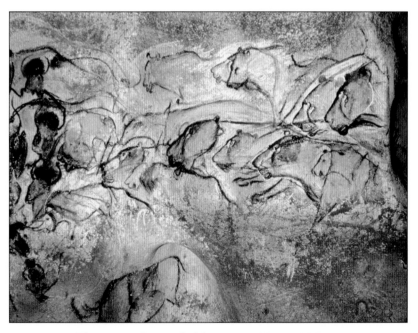

Plate 14. The *Panel of the Hunting Lions*, with bison (left), in the End Chamber, Chauvet cave.

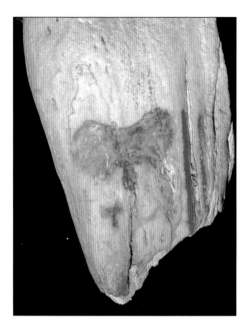

Plate 15.
Wide and narrow
signs from the
Chauvet cave.

Plate 16.
The composite
image of *The
Sorcerer* from the
End Chamber at
the Chauvet cave,
drawn by the
artist Thomas
Barron.

14

The Sign of the Hand

EARLY IN THE TWENTIETH CENTURY, A STRANGE CAVE was discovered in the central part of the French Pyrenees, not far from Lourdes. At this cave, called Gargas, almost all of the prehistoric art consisted of images of human hands, in red and black—some "negatives," stenciled hand images created by splashing paint around hands held to the cave wall, and others obtained by smearing hands with paint and stamping images on the walls.

The hand images found here are similar to the few hands found at Pech Merle. The art at Pech Merle was dated to about the Last Glacial Maximum (22,000 years ago). But Gargas is an even older cave. We now know from radiocarbon analysis that the art in this cave is far more ancient—it is of the same period as the Chauvet cave, 31,000 to 27,000 years ago.

Images of hands were found in the deep recesses of this cave, and, in particular, one was placed in a natural niche in the cave, while others were tilted at various angles. These hands were of various sizes; some hands had belonged to men and women and others to children. Some hands appeared to be mutilated—lacking certain fingers. Henri Breuil developed a theory to address this mystery. He hypothesized a Cro-Magnon cult of mutilation.

But why were there so many hands at Gargas, and why were they all of different sizes, belonging to both men and women and with different numbers of fingers showing? No one had an answer to this riddle, but a recent analysis revealed that Breuil may have been wrong. An experiment was carried out, showing that normal hands could have been drawn in such a way as to match images in this cave—without their actually being mutilated. This, of course, does not prove that the hands in the Gargas prints were not mutilated or otherwise missing fingers.

Yet the idea of mutilation in a society that depended on able-bodied people for hunting and gathering is bizarre. And at Gargas, many hands appear mutilated. One competing theory is that the cold weather of the Ice Age caused frequent frostbite, which then led to lost fingers, rather than active mutilation.[1] This is certainly a plausible hypothesis, although, as experiments have shown, perhaps bent fingers were used here to create a code, and none of the fingers were actually mutilated. It should be noted that hands that appear mutilated have been found only in Gargas; the hands that made prints in other caves appear to have been intact.

The most promising theory was proposed by André Leroi-Gourhan in his seminal treatise, Le fil du temps (The Thread of Time), first published in 1957 (and reissued in 1983). It explained the mysterious code that he believed was the purpose of the hand signs at Gargas. The following analysis is based on Leroi-Gourhan's results.[2]

Leroi-Gourhan rejected Breuil's hypothesis that there was some kind of ritual mutilation of people's hands. He argued that the variety and the kinds of missing or deformed fingers make the hypothesis unlikely. He further noted that 50 percent of all handprints at Gargas show no fingers other than the thumb, which he found extraordinary under an assumption of mutilation.

Leroi-Gourhan then took up the hypothesis of lost fingers due to frostbite and gangrene, as well as genetic pathologies or nutritional deficiencies. This hypothesis was also entertained by Breuil and developed further by a number of French medical experts. But again, the placement of missing fingers, according to Leroi-Gourhan, makes this hypothesis equally unlikely. Leroi-Gourhan next brought a key element into the analysis. He argued that under either hypothesis, there would have been some degree of randomness in the pattern of which fingers were missing from the hands. Here, he claimed, he could show that the handprints at Gargas are not random—they fit particular structures. This hypothesis, according to Leroi-Gourhan, was first proposed by P. Saintyves in 1934.[3] Yet the theory was still in its rudimentary stages until Leroi-Gourhan saved it from obscurity and developed it further.

Leroi-Gourhan has shown that it is possible with bent fingers, placing a palm or the back of the hand against a wall and using paints similar to those used by the Paleolithic people, to reproduce all of the hand signs at Gargas. He then went on to classify the hand signs by type, depending on how many fingers are shown and which ones are missing. He assigned each type of handprint a letter designation: A, B, C, up to O. A straight hand with five fingers showing appears twelve times in the cave (A); a hand with the first finger bent (or missing) appears three times (B); a hand with the middle finger missing or bent appears thirteen times (C).

As a starting point, Leroi-Gourhan noted that combinations of missing fingers that are hard to make with a hand are rarely depicted. More often, none of the fingers (only the thumb) are shown—combination "O," which is the most frequently occurring—or those that have one or two fingers missing, or none ("A").

In the next step of his analysis, Leroi-Gourhan studied combinations of hands in various parts of the cave. He found that the most common combination was that of the letters, in order, OACHNK, a combination that is easy to make. Another easy ordered combination, BEFG, however, is rare. Series of contiguous fingers were apparently preferred, which makes the assumptions of mutilation or natural finger loss much less likely.

Finally, Leroi-Gourhan studied the colors of the hands. Here he found a stunning pattern: the frequency of hand colors changed uniformly from the cave entrance to the cave depths. The hands appear in two colors: red or black. At the entrance to the cave, the red hands make up 22 percent of the total (the rest are black). As one proceeds into the next gallery, the proportion of red hands goes up to 25 percent. It continues to rise arithmetically and uniformly until we reach the depths of the cave. Here the proportion of red hands is 58 percent. Leroi-Gourhan argued that such a pattern must have carried some meaning and was unlikely to have arisen purely by chance.[4]

The hand signs at Gargas and elsewhere in the Pyrenees and the Dordogne, as well as in Spain, are by all likelihood not random. This had to have been a code of some kind, but its meaning still eludes modern science. In the final analysis reported in his study, Leroi-Gourhan found an intriguing connection between hand signs at Gargas and the types of animals painted, drawn, or carved in other caves. For the caves of the Pyrenees, the following association was discovered:[5]

Hand Sign	Percentage	Animal Drawn	Percentage
O	47	Bison	49
A	17	Horse	28
C	14	Ibex	6
H	7.5	Deer	4
Other	14.5	Other	13

Leroi-Gourhan hypothesized an identification of hand sign O with the bison; A with the horse; C with the ibex; and H with the deer. It should be noted, however, that there is no statistical or scientific proof of such a hypothesis. But it is certainly an intriguing possibility.

. . .

The cave of Gargas lies in an unassuming spot in the lower reaches of the central Pyrenees in France. This wooded area is not thickly settled; the roads are narrow and there is little traffic. Some miles to the east lies the little medieval town of Saint Bertrand de Commings. This is a charming yet not well-known medieval walled hill town with an imposing cathedral that was built in the thirteenth century. Below the town are extensive Roman ruins, including a theater and baths. These were surprising, because they looked almost intact. It seems that we don't need a volcano, as in the case of Pompeii, to preserve Roman ruins in excellent condition. But this was not what I came here for—I had made the trip to the central Pyrenees (Niaux is in the eastern part of the mountain chain) to visit the cave of Gargas.

The trip from Saint Bertrand to the cave of Gargas took only a few minutes by car. Parking was amply available there, and we could easily sign up for the next tour—something that would be impossible to do at many other Paleolithic caves. It's a shame that this remarkable cave doesn't draw as many tourists as it should; perhaps this is due to its isolated location.

After entering the cave, we followed the slippery path marked by electric lightbulbs that showed the way. We passed several stalagmites and stalactites. As we walked into the first gallery, we were stunned by the number of handprints there. We saw a few paintings of animals, but most of the images were black or red handprints. Some were outlined, while others were stamped prints. Then we followed the guide into the depths of the cave—a location where, in most other decorated caves, one would find the most elaborate, most artistic display of animals. But at Gargas, instead, there was a large concentration of red hands and, in the very center, a niche.

This was a recessed area in the rock, and as our guide shone her light on it, we could see in the center of the niche one large, straight-facing black hand. This seemed to be the core of everything in this mysterious cave: all other art and handprints seemed to revolve around "the hand in the niche." What this hand means remains a deep mystery, but it certainly is not random and was placed there by design. Someone who entered this deep cavern 27,000 years ago (as determined by radiocarbon analysis) wanted a large hand—not a bison or a horse—to be the central piece in this strange gallery.

Our guide kept us here in suspense, looking at the large hand. She told us that this central hand sign had been so puzzling to scientists that they invited present-day hunter-gatherers to offer their explanations. They brought in an African San tribesman from the Kalahari and also an Australian aborigine to look at the hand. Both men, from societies that live oceans apart, gave the same explanation: This hand, as they interpreted it according to their own traditions, was a representation of people reaching for the world beyond. The deepest part of the cave is the end of our world, both men said. The hand is reaching for what lies beyond the cave, beyond our world, and is found in the realm of the dead and the ever-after.

As we left the cave, I talked to our guide. She was very knowledgeable, as well as enthusiastic, about her work and prehistory and the cave of Gargas. I knew about Breuil's work here, and since our guide had mentioned him during our visit, I offered my interpretation of his theory. "Breuil believed there was a religious significance to it all, even the hand signs here, right?" I asked. "But of course," she answered. "You couldn't expect otherwise from him—he was an Abbé!"

15

The Legend of the White Lady

IN 1485, THE GREAT PORTUGUESE NAVIGATOR DIEGO CÃO placed his most southerly stone pillar commemorating his arrival at a location on the West African coast at 21 degrees, 50 minutes south. But, seeing no sign of humans, Cão did not proceed inland and missed discovering the towering Brandberg Mountain. This granite massif rises straight up from the desert floor. There are no water holes here, so travel may be dangerous; there are minor veins of copper and gold, crags, and deep ravines.

Centuries later, this land of the Namib Desert, now called Namibia, was colonized by Germany, and many of the white settlers here still speak German. In 1920, the German explorer Lieutenant Hugo Jochmann came upon rock paintings high on the slopes of the Brandberg. But he failed to find the greatest and most mysterious of all, one that would be called the *White Lady* of Africa. Jochmann and his colleagues overlooked this unusual ancient artwork because it was well hidden inside a natural rock alcove into which direct sunlight never reaches. A narrow passage on a terrace above a ravine leads to the painting's hiding place. The artists who created this beguiling painting apparently took pains to hide it in a way that is reminiscent of the Cro-Magnons of France and Spain.

Three years earlier, in 1917, a German topographer named Reinhardt Maack was working up on the Brandberg. He lost contact with his coworkers, ran out of food and water, and was unable to return. Desperately looking for a way down the mountain, the famished Maack fell into the alcove and discovered to his astonishment the painting of the *White Lady*. In his notebook, he drew some sketches of this amazing painting. Maack was saved and in 1920 visited the site again. In 1929, his notebook, bearing the reproductions of the *White Lady*, was brought to the attention of Henri Breuil in Paris.

After inspecting this strange painting, Breuil requested through friends in southern Africa that Dr. E. Scherz of Windhoek, Namibia, make a trip to the Brandberg and photograph the painting. These photographs were brought to Breuil in 1937, and he could finally see what the *White Lady* actually looked like. He was captivated by it and decided to visit southern Africa to inspect this intriguing painting.

In 1942, Breuil came to Johannesburg, and at the Archaeological Survey laboratory he was shown an enlargement of the photographs made by Scherz. But even before he saw the actual rock painting and the photographs, Breuil made a stunning and controversial determination:

> Maack's sketch of the White Lady of the Brandberg revealed to me both the site itself and the existence in South-West Africa of an art very superior to that of the Bushmen. It is the art of

a red-haired people (with Semitic profiles) who painted hundreds of rock shelters. The picture of the White Lady of the Tsisab seems to me to be the crowning glory of this art.[1]

In 1947, Breuil returned to Africa, and this time he made the trek all the way up the Brandberg, climbing to an elevation of 8,200 feet, with guides, and was shown the *White Lady*. He was seventy years old now, but the old cave explorer was tireless. He camped at the foot of the rock bearing the great painting and at night heard lions roaming around. But Breuil was unfazed, and during the next fifteen days he drew a careful reproduction of the painting, as he had done so many times in European caves. In addition to the Bushmen (now called the San people) guides, Breuil was accompanied by Dr. Scherz and two other scientists from South Africa. The others took photographs that would be used along with Breuil's reproduction.

Breuil returned to the *White Lady* twice more: in 1948 and in 1950. During his long visits and analyses, he further developed his theory about the provenance and meaning of the painting, which he believed to have been made around 1500 BC.

Breuil concluded that the *White Lady* had been painted in eleven layers of paint. The eleventh layer was a polychrome depiction of a symbolic ceremonial procession. As Broderick described it,

> There are animals, eland, oryx, springbok, an antelope with man's arms and legs, an oryx with human hindquarters, a hartebeest with human hindlegs, a man with a crocodile's head, a white man disguised as a baboon; there are twenty-eight human figures, including the crocodile-man, musicians, and others, steatopygous women; the

procession is led by two youths who, like the
crocodile-man, are infibulated.

The White Lady herself is striding along
toward the left; she holds up to her face either
a cup or a large white flower, in her left hand
stretched out behind her she has a strung bow
and arrows, and a sheaf of three more. From
waist to feet she is rosy-white while from waist to
neck she is covered in some dark-colored, cling-
ing garment, with short sleeves and embroidered
with several bands of beads. The face is very
delicately painted and is, Breuil considered, of
"Mediterranean" type; in any case it is not Negro
or "African."

Behind her is an uncanny figure, dark in
color, the tallest of all. On his dusky face is
painted in white a lower jaw complete with teeth
and also an eye socket, in fact, his head is a skull.
He is infibulated . . . and then after him are two
red-haired young people running . . . and still
more figures.[2]

The *White Lady* is the most enigmatic of the rock paintings
of Africa. Breuil believed that the figures in the painting are a
mixture of races. Some were African, but the *White Lady* herself is not only drawn in white, but her facial features are indeed
non-African and do bear an eerie resemblance to the women
depicted in frescoes discovered in archaeological excavations of
Minoan sites: at the palace of Knossos on Crete or at Akrotiri
on the island of Santorini. The Abbé wrote, "My opinion is that
a mixed group of foreigners, mixed when they were recruited,
in the course of their journeying added to their company Negro
servants, also foreign to the region, and that they brought with

them beliefs such as found in Egypt and Crete. . . . [T]he Lady's costume is obviously Cretan."[3]

Breuil's contention is outlandish. Does it bear any scholarly consideration? An inspection of the *White Lady* will reveal a resemblance to frescoes found on Minoan sites on Crete (Knossos and Phaestos) and on the Greek island of Santorini, both remnants of the ancient Minoan civilization believed to have been the model for the lost Atlantis of legend—an advanced civilization that suddenly disappeared off the face of the Earth. We now know that the cause of that calamity was the massive explosion of the Santorini volcano around 1628 BC. Had the survivors of the Minoan civilization, known to have been great mariners, made it to the southwest coast of Africa and settled there long before Cão arrived in the fifteenth century?

• • •

In 1932, the Greek archaeologist Spyridon Marinatos was excavating at the site of Amnisos, the harbor that served the great palace of Knossos on Crete. Marinatos was working at a relatively high point near what had been the harbor, excavating the remains of a Minoan villa. What he discovered struck him as bizarre. The villa seemed to have been pulled right off its foundations by some mysterious force.

As Marinatos began to notice similar signs of unexplained destruction at other sites on Crete, he became convinced that the Minoan civilization did not come to its end through war, economic competition, or natural decline—or any other conventional way. The Minoans were the victims of a sinister natural force of unprecedented scale. But what was it? Marinatos was one of the most imaginative archaeologists of all time. He was able to interpret clues in his archaeological finds on the ground and from them draw broad conclusions about the major events that caused them. He was a big-picture visionary who could collect many small pieces of information to create a wide vision of the world around us and our distant past.

In 1939, Marinatos published an article titled "The Volcanic Destruction of Minoan Crete" in the English periodical *Antiquity*. In it, he proposed his theory that a violent eruption of the Santorini volcano had destroyed the Minoan civilization on the island of Crete. According to Marinatos, the eruption was accompanied by violent earthquakes that caused great tidal waves. The Minoan settlements on Crete were destroyed by the tidal waves and by large amounts of volcanic ash deposited on the land, which made any agriculture impossible. But Atlantis is not the only legend we have about the total and sudden destruction of a human civilization by forces of nature.

A short time after Marinatos had first started to excavate south of the village of Akrotiri on Santorini Island in 1967, his team made an incredible discovery. An entire ancient city lay under the ash and pumice, just like Pompeii. But this one was seventeen centuries older. Two-storied houses with running water and flushing toilets lined the streets and a city square. Inside these houses, Marinatos's team found elaborate frescoes and beautiful vases crafted by artisans of a civilization that later disappeared suddenly and without explanation. Marinatos's work received worldwide media attention, and the *National Geographic*, which in 1967 published stunning pictures of the frescoes and art treasures recovered at Akrotiri, described his work as the unearthing of Atlantis.

Tantalizingly, frescoes found at Akrotiri bear a striking resemblance to animal depictions in Paleolithic caves in France and Spain. Here, too, many thousands of years after the end of the Paleolithic era, animals are drawn without terrain, and sometimes they overlap.

Among the disasters attributed to the Santorini eruption, some have counted the Ten Plagues of Egypt and the Parting of the Sea. The assumption has been that the eruption caused the three days of darkness described in the Bible, and that the remaining plagues were secondary effects of the same event. The Parting of the Sea has been attributed to the tidal wave that resulted from the Santorini eruption. Marinatos himself cared only about the Atlantis legend and was never a proponent of the Ten Plagues and Parting of the Sea hypothesis.

Tragically, Marinatos fell to his death on site at Akrotiri in 1974. Thus, the immensely important archaeological and historical work he had been doing, revealing the mysteries of our past, came to an end. The cause of his death was reported by the Greek media as a stroke that led to his losing his balance on the high ledge on which he was standing. To honor the great achievements of this leader in archaeology, people buried his body on site at Akrotiri, right next to where he fell. Fresh flowers are still placed there daily.

• • •

I had studied the disappearance of the Minoan civilization when I was a scientist working on radiocarbon dates from Crete and Santorini. As part of my research, I traveled to the Aegean to inspect some of the finds.

How did the catastrophe of the eruption affect people? This was something I often wondered about while doing my technical work on statistical methods to improve the radiocarbon dating technique. I used an advanced mathematical method called the "bootstrap" to obtain a narrow confidence interval for radiocarbon dates of prehistoric events.

As part of this project, I also wanted to visit the site of the most devastating natural calamity in human history—the place where archaeologists had found the remains of an ancient civilization that had mysteriously vanished around 1628 BC. Among the archaeological finds were jars containing grains of barley left by the people who had died in this great disaster, and these grains were used in the radiocarbon dating.

A few days after I arrived on Santorini, I climbed to the top of the rim of the huge volcano. Near a terrace with a good view of the caldera below, I read a sign: "Trespassing for Customers Only." I chuckled and continued on my way, walking south for half an hour and then turning west. I rounded a sheltered area behind a small hill and was again facing the enormous blue caldera below me, this time looking north. It is from here, the southern rim of the volcano, that one can grasp the sheer size of the crater. It was a clear day, yet I could hardly see the northernmost town of Ia, directly across the caldera. The amount of earth and rocks blown into the air that day or during several days in the seventeenth century BC must have been enormous.

All around me were large black basalt rocks. They looked as if they had fallen out of the sky and landed scattered over the yellow-gray earth. The same northerly wind must have been blowing then, when the eruption occurred (as has been proved by studies of ash in deep-sea cores), and the rocks, the ash, and the pumice caused a hellish devastation as the wind swept them in the air to the south and the east. A thick layer of ash covered the fields of Crete, seventy miles to the south. Modern science has shown that if volcanic ash covers arable land to the depth discovered on Crete, it will make such land unsuitable for human use for many years.

The strong winds carried the enormous cloud of ash and debris southeast toward Egypt, where it caused darkness that wouldn't lift for days. As I was thinking of the cataclysm that took place so long ago, the sun was beating down on me and it was very hot and dry, but I finally made it to the entrance of the village of Akrotiri. From there, it was another half-hour's walk due south, descending the steep path to the water's edge on the south coast of the island.

Here was the archaeological site in which Marinatos had made his great discovery of a Minoan city with streets and two-story houses whose rooms were painted with beautiful frescoes and whose bathrooms had flushing toilets. I admired an intact house, built three and a half millennia ago, standing at the corner of an ancient street. I closed my eyes and imagined carts laden with goods moving on that street and people dressed in Minoan clothing and wearing the gold jewelry I'd seen on frescoes. When I opened my eyes again, I looked below me, down at the yard of this prehistoric house. It was then that I saw a large bunch of flowers carefully placed on a gravestone.

• • •

It was a Saturday night, and Panayotis and his wife and daughter dressed well. They wore the festive costumes of their island: embroidered white shirts and elegant blue trousers or skirts. "Tonight, we go together," Panayotis had said to me after breakfast that morning. I tried to dress as well as I could, but traveling with a small bag didn't allow for many possibilities. At seven, I met the three of them in the hallway. We climbed into the red minivan, the three of them up front and I in the back. Panayotis took the dusty, bumpy road from the town of Naxos to the mountain village of Filoti. We drove past cultivated fields and barren hills where a few sheep grazed. Panayotis and his family were happy, singing Greek songs.

In half an hour, we entered the well-lit square of the village. As we turned, a bearded man in his thirties who had been standing on the sidewalk near his car, ran into the street, smiling and waving. Panayotis stopped beside him, and the two men spoke excitedly in Greek. We parked and joined the man and his wife and daughter, and they all kissed one another and shook hands with me. "Synadelfos sas," said Panayotis as he introduced me to his friend. "Your colleague." Andreas was a professor of archaeology, and so in that sense we were colleagues, since Panayotis and his family knew that I was a professor.

Andreas didn't speak any English, but his twelve-year-old daughter, Eleni, proved to be a good translator. We entered the restaurant, everyone in a convivial mood. First came the *mezedes*, the hors d'oeuvres that tourists in Greece go crazy over: cucumber-yogurt salad, fish-egg salad, chopped octopus. Then pizza and bottles of retsina and red wine arrived. The conversation flowed. The two families were apparently very close, and I felt privileged to be invited to such an intimate outing.

"I was in Santorini," I said, once Andreas had finally turned to me with a question. "I was amazed to see Marinatos's grave— I hadn't known he was buried right there on site in Akrotiri, where he fell." Andreas smiled. "Oh, yes, Marinatos. He was a wonderful archaeologist," he said. "But he didn't just fall. Marinatos was murdered." I looked at him, stupefied. *Murdered?* Eleni was translating word for word as he spoke. "You didn't know?" he asked. "The people didn't like all of those theories that were coming out because of his work. You know, about the parting of the sea and the plagues of Egypt. The workers Marinatos had with him on site were very religious people. And they were also primitive and superstitious. To them, it all had to be the work of God—not a volcano. They had to kill him, to stop the blasphemy."

• • •

Breuil's intriguing theory about a possible connection between the lost Minoan civilization of the eastern Mediterranean and a single rock painting on a mountaintop in the desert of southern Africa cannot be dismissed offhand. The Abbé knew very well the theories about Atlantis and was well aware of the findings from Crete that had been made by his time. He had studied Minoan art, as well as all of the prehistoric cave art of Europe. His theory attracted some obvious interest. But it was not politically correct, and it ruffled quite a few feathers.

Some modern-day experts believe that the *White Lady* of Africa is a man, and that he is African, not Mediterranean. They assume he is a shaman, dressed in white, moving among herds of animals and a group of hunters. Shamanism is practiced by present-day tribes in Africa; hence this deduction. The painting of the *White Lady* is part of a collection of forty-five thousand rock-art pieces featuring animals and people found on the slopes of Brandberg Mountain in Namibia, and the *White Lady* is at the top, at an altitude of 8,200 feet above sea level. These animal paintings resemble in many ways the animals painted on cave walls in France and Spain, and Breuil hypothesized a connection between the two art forms.

But Breuil had studied almost exclusively European cave art, and critics contended that perhaps he had developed a cultural bias: was he unable to imagine a good prehistoric artist as anything but a Caucasian? Was it a bias that led him to the bizarre theory that Europeans had traveled to Africa many thousands of years ago, and that these people, or their descendents—racially different from the African natives of this area—had created the rock-art masterpiece? Someday, perhaps radiocarbon analysis (if it is possible) may reveal clues about the origin of the *White Lady* of Africa.

Breuil's views proved too much for Europeans to bear, and his reputation suffered. People were able to see that the flaws in his thinking and interpretation might also extend to his view about the purpose of European cave art. It was time for a change. Breuil died in 1961, and eight years later, his chaired position at the Collège de France was given to a gifted prehistorian who would leave an indelible mark on our view of the mystery of the caves—André Leroi-Gourhan.

• • •

According to Jean Clottes,

> Years later, the rock art specialist Harald Pager began working in the Brandberg. He devoted his life to the task of studying and carefully tracing tens of thousands of San rock paintings in southern Africa. Pager's copy of the White Lady revealed that the head is African and the figure has a penis. It is in fact a San male. Other studies since have confirmed Pager's analysis. The shelter has kept its original name, even though, as the renowned scholar David Lewis-Williams has famously remarked, the White Lady of the Brandberg "is neither white nor a lady."[4]

But Clottes often tries to discredit Breuil, who, like Leroi-Gourhan, had great vision, which perhaps Clottes lacks. And he seems eager to plug for his colleague and coauthor Lewis-Williams. It is hard to see how one can determine, based on the

image of the *White Lady*, why the head is
African, and where, exactly, he sees a penis.
None is evident from looking at the image—if
there is one, it is microscopically small. This
becomes evident from inspecting the image
of the *White Lady* in Plate 8.

And let's not forget that the Abbé had
spent many days studying the *White Lady*,
long before it faded after so many visitors
splashed her with water to make the color

Plate 8. The *White
Lady* of Africa.

come out for better photography (that practice is now forbidden). Surely, Breuil would have noticed the penis if the *White
Lady* had one. And the Abbé's opinion that the *White Lady*
resembles Minoan women from frescoes found on Crete and
Akrotiri does seem plausible: the clothing, the hairstyle, the
facial features, the jewelry, and the way her body is positioned
certainly could pass for Minoan. The hypothesis Breuil put forward is interesting, and it merits further study.

Despite virulent criticism, the Abbé stood his ground. And
when in 1956 he wrote his masterpiece, *Four Hundred Centuries of Cave Art*—a book dedicated to Paleolithic European
cave art—he chose to begin it with his story of the *White Lady*
of Africa. Poetically, Breuil wrote,

> Ah yes, dear friends and readers, he who pres-
> ents this book has come from the far end of
> Africa where, painted in the hollow of the rock,
> thousands of years ago, a very ancient young girl
> awaited him. Eternally she walks there, young,
> beautiful and supple, almost aerian in poise. In
> ancient times, all her own people also walked
> to contemplate her adored image and all went

on walking for centuries, not only men, but the oryxes, spring buck, ostriches, giraffes, elephants and rhinoceros swayed by her magic. In my turn, it was for her sake I walked, urged forward since the day when, from a poor sketch made by her exhausted discoverer, I gazed on her face. One day she drew me from the somber gloom of our European caverns, and the great Jan Smuts sent me toward her, in the fierce sunshine of Damaraland. Across deserts, we walked towards her. I and my friends and guides, captivated by her incomparable grace; I tried to record her features. Three times I returned to see her. I brought other companions and spoke of her to the world of the living, after having once more dreamed at her feet of the infinite mystery in the history of ancient migrations. To her, to her companions, to her people, known to us only from other frescoes, I have devoted several of the precious years that remain to me. There I learned a kind of marvelous gospel which it now seems to me opportune to declare in this troubled world, that of the living importance of those splendors, useless in material life and so essential in the life of the spirit. . . . Our White Lady has brought this precious message down a very far road, stammered at first by our Reindeer Age painters, nearly 40,000 years ago. It is thanks to this that Man the Artist, rising above the rough stone workers, who, at the beginning, had no art, became the being in love with progress, perfection, and beauty.[5]

Through the work and thought of Henri Breuil, the real-world Indiana Jones of prehistory, an intriguing painting on a rock on a high mountain in southern Africa remains forever linked with the Mediterranean world and with the cave artists of the Old Stone Age.

16

Shamans of the Tundra

In the mid-twentieth century, anthropology and prehistory united in the quest for a solution to the riddle of the cave art. What was the motivation for, and the purpose of, this art? Once the mighty Henri Breuil was doubted, people began to look elsewhere for hints on how to solve this enduring mystery. The animals that were the subjects of Paleolithic cave art were clearly not those that were most often hunted. In addition, most of the painted or drawn animals look happy and alive. The ibex found on the Grand Ceiling of the cave of Rouffignac seem so content, they appear to be smiling. Other animals prance around in space in a way that makes it obvious the artists didn't want to kill them. The jumping cow of Lascaux looks very lively; the bulls of Altamira are in a mating frenzy; the horses of Pech Merle are regal. None of these animals are drawn as if the artists simply wanted to make a meal out of them. Does the noble-looking Pyrenean ibex of Niaux, drawn in such marvelous detail, with head high and bright eye looking right at the observer, appear as if it's about to become a dinner of lamb chops?

. . .

The proportions of the kinds of animals depicted in cave art in France and Spain have been tabulated, and these numbers may contain clues about the art. These calculations would be exploited by André Leroi-Gourhan in developing his theory about the purpose and meaning of cave art. Although Leroi-Gourhan did his work in the 1950s and has since died, the important cave of Chauvet and a few others have been discovered since his death. The following table, obtained from statistical abstracts on cave art, incorporates the information about animal depictions (paintings, drawings, and engravings) in all known caves.[1] The table shows the percentage of each animal image as compared with a total of 3,558 artistic animal depictions in all known decorated caves in France and Spain as of the present.

Animal	Percentage	Number of Cases
Horse	27.5	981
Bison	21	750
Ibex	9	322
Mammoth	8.2	294
Aurochs	5.8	209
Deer	5.5	196
Reindeer	3.7	123
Lion	2.1	77
Rhinoceros	2	71
Bear	1.7	47
Other (including birds and fish)	<1	

It is important to understand the following facts. Some of the animals that appear rarely, as seen in the context of the totality of Franco-Cantabrian caves, may show up in relative abundance in any given cave. Thus, for example, lions are rare overall, but they appear relatively frequently in the Chauvet cave—even as a group of sub-

Plate 9. The hunting lions of Chauvet cave.

limely drawn hunting lions, shown in Plate 9. Plates 10 through 15 are also breathtaking drawings from the Chauvet cave.

Plate 10. A rhinoceros from Chauvet cave.

Plate 11. The beautiful horses of Chauvet cave.

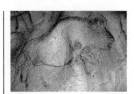

Plate 12. A bison from Chauvet cave.

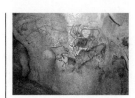

Plate 13. A panel with many animals, Chauvet cave.

Plate 14. The *Panel of the Hunting Lions*, also showing other animals, Chauvet cave.

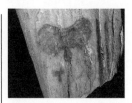

Plate 15. Wide and narrow signs from Chauvet cave.

At Rouffignac, for example, mammoths are relatively frequent, whereas overall they account for only 8.2 percent of depicted animals. But the key point here is that in *all* caves, the horse and the bison are the leading animals—in their roles, their prominence, and their relative numbers. The percentages of these two animals dominate not only overall, but also in most caves individually. Leroi-Gourhan was led to believe that the horse and the bison were somehow paired, and that all other animals were merely filling the roles of supporting characters in the great drama played out in Paleolithic cave art in Europe. But what did the horse and the bison mean, and what were the supporting roles of the other animals? Leroi-Gourhan would develop an entire theory around his hypothesis.

• • •

In the meantime, others, who were perhaps less gifted and had less vision and imagination, tried to proffer their own views about what the animal paintings and the signs in European caves meant. In particular, modern anthropological research proposed a direction in which to look.

Anthropologists offered their help and brought in the results of studies of present-day populations that live in faraway locations such as the Siberian tundra. These Eskimos and other native peoples live on hunting, and the anthropological assumption has been that perhaps these peoples' cultures were not too different from those of the European Cro-Magnons, whose terrain during the Ice Age consisted of similar tundra and permafrost, and who also subsisted on hunting and gathering. This seemed a very reasonable assumption—one that could logically lead to an inference from present-day Siberia and the

Kalahari to the Dordogne, Pyrenees, and Cantabria two hundred centuries ago.

The present-day northern hunters practice shamanism. A shaman is a priest who uses magic to cure the sick, divine hidden truths, and control the future. Often, the shaman uses herbal hallucinogens to cause a trance, which is considered essential for his purposes. Shamanist societies believe in an unseen world of gods, demons, and ancestral spirits that respond to the shaman when he performs his magic and enters a state of heightened consciousness. Anthropologists surmised that the cave painters were shamans, and that they performed their art under the influence of such herbal concoctions.

The main proponents of this theory were the French prehistorian Jean Clottes, who was born and raised in the Pyrenees and had explored the caves in this region throughout his life, and his South African colleague David Lewis-Williams. The latter had studied rock art in the Western Cape Province of South Africa, as well as the lives of hunter-gatherers in the Kalahari (where, as on the northern tundra, a form of shamanism is practiced), and he became convinced that shamanism was the salient element of tribal culture in South Africa.

In their joint book *The Shamans of Prehistory (Les chamanes de la préhistoire* [Paris: La Maison des Roches, 1993; reissued with commentary, 2001]), the pair argued for a shamanistic interpretation of the motivation for European cave art. A finding that helped them support their thesis was the discovery in a couple of French caves of what may look like "sorcerer" drawings. These are drawings of figures that appear anthropomorphic but have some animal elements—a human body with a stag's head and horns, for example. The authors knew that the northern tundra shamans often wore animal furs and antlers to make them look like animals, and so they deduced that the strange, isolated, mixed drawings indeed represented prehistoric shamans.

In the cave of Trois Frères in the Pyrenees there is a drawing of a man-deer, whom prehistorians have dubbed *The Little Sorcerer*. It is a depiction of what looks like a man, with what is clearly a human torso and human feet, but with an upper body of a stag. Is this an imaginary creature—of which there are several examples in Paleolithic cave art, such as the Lascaux "unicorn"—or is it a man dressed in a stag's mask with horns? The answer is unknown. And even if it were known, would it necessarily be a shaman? It could just as well be a hunter disguising himself as an animal. There is also a Magdalenian statuette found at an archaeological site in Germany that is human below the waist and has a lion's head. Is this a shaman?

The theory of Clottes and Lewis-Williams rested in a crucial way on the interpretation of these depictions as clear representations of prehistoric shamans, taken hand in hand with anthropological evidence from present-day societies in Siberia and South Africa.

But could the wonderfully detailed paintings and drawings of animals have been made by an artist who was in a drug-induced trance? According to experts in botany, plants containing known hallucinogens were not found in the regions of Paleolithic decorated caves during the Ice Age. And what about the multitude of *signs* found in caves—what did they mean within the shamanistic context?

Clottes has lived a somewhat charmed life. Born and raised in a region rich in prehistoric caves, he could explore them at leisure—even before he earned his PhD at age forty-one and assumed a leadership position in French prehistory.[2] He has been exceptionally privileged to be able to join France's intellectual elite once he had made significant scholarly contributions, and in this new role he has been in a position to obtain access to all of France's prehistoric treasures. In a sense, Clottes became Breuil's successor—he gained the right to enter and work in any Paleolithic cave he desired, and he was the leader of the team that explored Chauvet after its discovery.

But it is difficult to judge the extent of Clottes's vision. Is he an intellectual at the level of the great Henri Breuil? If nothing else, I find that even if the shamanistic interpretation is partly true—and I don't believe it is—it trivializes what are clearly unprecedented artistic achievements. After Clottes's inspecting so many caves filled with rich, meaningful art, is his answer that it was all created because of shamanism a satisfying one? Would Clottes's theory gain scientific verification? Perhaps the two human figures dressed as animals had something to do with the practice, but to say that all of this amazing artistic activity was merely a by-product of shamanism debases the wonderful art. The theory also sounds too simple and perhaps naive. The scientific community has not overwhelmingly embraced the neo-shamanistic hypothesis. One biting criticism even called the Clottes and Lewis-Williams theory the result of a "dumb brain."[3] Is it?

• • •

Alaska has native Eskimo and Indian tribes. Shamanism is believed to be practiced in Siberia, and the connections between native populations in Siberia and Alaska are strong, in terms of the development of culture on both sides of the Bering Sea. In fact, the Diomede Islands, one in Alaska and the other in Siberia, are especially close to each other, their separate populations mixing together. It was with this cultural assumption in mind that I went to Alaska to investigate native cultures and a possible shamanistic connection.

My plane left Fairbanks, in the center of Alaska, late in the evening on February 13. Just before midnight, I landed on the frozen airstrip of Barrow, the northernmost settlement in the United States—an Eskimo village on the shores of the Arctic Ocean at 71 degrees north. It was minus 38 degrees Fahrenheit when I walked from the plane to the small terminal building, bracing myself against a wind that made the cold almost impossible to bear. At this low temperature and extreme wind chill, unprotected human skin freezes in less than a minute. My eyes watered as I entered the building, and I tried to warm myself up before again facing the brutal cold for the walk across the street and around a corner to the North of the Border Hotel. It was the only lodging in the village, located right on the beach of the Arctic Ocean, which was solidly frozen with jagged blocks of ice jutting over the surface.

Barrow wasn't the safest place in the world, either. I had heard that a .357 Magnum was the weapon of choice in the village, owned by almost every man who lived there (and some of the women as well), and I knew that the Eskimos here were notoriously intolerant of strangers, especially those who were not native Alaskan. A young white man had been shot to death on the street here two weeks earlier, for no apparent reason.

It was just after midnight when I entered the hotel and obtained the key to my room. I was happy to have made the reservation—had I not done so, I would have been in dire straits on this dangerously cold night. The hotel had very few rooms; visitors are rare in this native Alaskan village, especially in the dead of winter. After putting my things away, I went outside again. The excitement of being here was great, and I wanted to walk on the ice of the Arctic Ocean. I could hear the echo of my footsteps from the water below the surface ice. It was a clear dark night, and as I took a few more steps away from the shore, I looked up and saw the most awesome display of northern lights above me: shimmering waves of red, yellow, and green fluorescence swept the entire canopy of the night sky. I stood and watched in amazement, all alone at the top of the world.

The next morning, after a breakfast of reindeer sausage and black coffee, I headed for Barrow's high school. Because of the Alaska pipeline and the oil, which is owned by the state and the native corporations—which were established as a result of the Alaska Native Claims Settlement Act of 1971—Barrow is a wealthy village. The Eskimos made a wise decision some decades ago to invest their money in education. As a result, the high school is the most prominent building in the village, and it is here that town meetings take place. Classrooms are super-modern and even include a state-of-the-art television and movie-production studio. Kevin B., a local teacher, had invited me to visit and to interview students and their families about their culture.

As soon as I entered the classroom, however, I realized that Eskimo culture favors traditional activities such as fishing, whaling, and hunting over all else. The students seemed bright but uninterested in what the teacher was doing. They preferred to talk about a polar bear that had just been shot a couple of days earlier and to play catch with pencils and erasers thrown around the room. My interviews with the students and their families revealed a society that was very close to nature. The Eskimos love and revere animals—perhaps the way I imagine the Cro-Magnons did. And their artists carve images of whales and seals on harpoons, knife handles, and sheaves.

In contrast with the art of the caves, however, and with modern painting, Eskimo art is essentially an art of *objects*. The Eskimos and other native peoples of Alaska and northern Canada decorate many items of everyday use. In Barrow, and later in other villages in the interior of Alaska, I saw many such decorated objects: statuettes, pendants, knife and harpoon handles, and masks.

The variety of decorated items in Eskimo culture is impressive: it seems that almost every item of daily use is decorated in some way. The statuettes often depict people or animals, the most common being whales, seals, bears, birds, and walruses. These are carved in minute detail out of animal bones, soapstone, gypsum, or walrus ivory. The tradition of decorating everyday objects with drawings of animals and of carving statuettes and making masks goes back thousands of years. Museums of Eskimo art, such as those in Fairbanks, Alaska, and Ottawa, Canada, contain many such art objects dating from a thousand years ago or earlier.

Some of the items are known to be as old as 500 BC, and scholars believe that there has never been a period since that time in which Eskimo artistic activity has stopped or disappeared.[4] But Eskimo art before that time is unknown, and it is likely that it began to be practiced by the Bering Sea communities of Alaska (that is, communities that existed southwest of Barrow, on the Bering Sea coast) around 2,500 years ago.[5]

What was the motivation for this artistic productivity? Many items used in the daily lives of the Eskimos, such as knives, spears, and harpoons, have handles that were probably decorated to make them look more attractive. Today, the statuettes and the masks are valued for their esthetically pleasing qualities. But these items also have symbolic value: they represent various tribes, and some of them recall myths and historical tales of the arctic Eskimo peoples.

Yet I couldn't find any evidence for shamanism. Alaska natives believe that animals have souls, or spirits. The spirits seemed to be an abstract concept—perhaps not something to be conjured or manipulated, the way certain anthropologists view shamanistic traditions. And the Eskimo tradition itself didn't seem precise: it included vague notions of the spirits or the souls of the animal world.

I learned a lot about Alaska natives and their culture. These people still belong to tribes and live a traditional lifestyle, in which ancient customs of family and social behavior prevail. They practice an interesting art, and in fact the art focuses on animal images. The tribes are named after animals, such as the raven, the bear, the whale, and the eagle.

I was inspecting two beautifully carved ivory statuettes of a mother and a child, yellowed by the centuries, when I asked the old Eskimo woman who showed them to me how and when they had been made. "The shaman made them," she answered matter-of-factly. "The shaman?" I repeated incredulously. "Sure," she answered, "this was two hundred years ago." As I followed the trail of this mystery, I found that shamans were quite important in early Eskimo societies.

In the coded words of the Eskimos of Greenland, a shaman is "he who is half hidden."[6] This name captures various qualities of the shaman. He lives in the shadows, and he initiates young tribe members into his art in hiding. The shaman is a man of the hidden world: he brings up spirits of the dead, consults with deceased elders, and understands the world beneath our world.[7] Shamans do not belong to groups or clubs—they are solitary, and they compete with one another for work. Typically, a tribe will have one shaman, who will train an apprentice as a successor.

The shaman is also a craftsman or an artist, because he makes statuettes and masks, which he uses in the shamanistic session of conjuring spirits of the dead or harnessing the powers of the hidden world to aid his people in the hunt or in family or social matters. Shamans also try to heal the sick. In communicating with spirits to achieve their goals, Inuit shamans speak in tongues and perform dances and rituals. This is often done at night and in poorly lit areas, so that the shaman remains hidden. The shamanistic ritual is connected with the Inuit religion, in

that dances are often derived from common religious perfor-
mances. The shaman is a person with an unusual psychological
makeup, and there have been suggestions that some shamans
suffered from mental illnesses.[8]

Until the early part of the twentieth century, Eskimo statuettes and masks were used in shamanistic rituals.[9] But in northern Alaska this has not happened once since 1918, and today all
statuettes and masks have only artistic and symbolic value.

For many centuries until the last one, the carvers of ivory
and other statuettes, as well as the makers of the masks, were
the shamans. They used the art objects they created in performing rituals and conjuring spirits. But contact with the outside,
which had intensified by the turn of the twentieth century, led
to a gradual disappearance of shamanism—which was frowned
on by missionaries who arrived in the arctic. The last shaman of
the Bering Sea area, a man named Kuzshuktuk (which means
"water drop" in the Inuit language spoken there), died in the
influenza pandemic of 1918. He had just returned to the arctic
after being confined for ten years in a mental institution in the
lower United States.[10]

It appears that shamanism is—or at least was, until a hundred years ago—an important part of tribal life in the arctic,
from Siberia to Alaska, to northern Canada and Greenland.
Shamans performed services for their fellow tribesmen, in
which they provided information, attempted to heal the ill, and
presumed to connect living people with spirits. They were paid
for their services with meat, other foods, and valuable commodi-
ties within the barter economy of the arctic. Shamans used in
their practice statuettes and masks, which they or other people
had made.

In comparing Eskimo shamanism with what we know about
the Cro-Magnons, we need to look at the art itself. Eskimo

statuettes are depictions of people and animals. The Cro-Magnon statuettes are of animals or of female humans with prominent sexual characteristics. Although there are differences between the kinds of statuettes used in both societies, it is not easy to reject the hypothesis of shamanism based on statuettes and masks in the present-day (or recent) arctic, on the one hand, and those of the European Paleolithic era.

But as far as cave art is concerned—the fixed parietal art on the walls and the ceilings of deep caverns in France and Spain—I believe that the story is quite different. The cave art follows precise, predetermined rules of composition that do not vary over millennia. Intricately drawn animals overlap without any terrain, and humanlike figures are rare and only schematic in nature. There seems to be a deep inner structure to Paleolithic parietal art that is unlikely—in my estimation—to have occurred as the result of a shaman's requirements. So what is the meaning of the structure, and what is the purpose of this majestic art?

• • •

Breuil made the first serious modern effort to understand cave art. After volumes of his work had been published in the first half of the twentieth century, many questions persisted about the meaning of the cave art and signs. In any eventuality, two competing theories were born from the ashes of Breuil's interpretation and survived well into the twentieth century: one was the shamanistic interpretation of cave art, and the other was that the paintings and the drawings were simply art for art's sake. According to this view, now championed and further developed by Ian Tattersall, the prehistoric artists created their magnificent paintings and drawings because they could—because they were excited by their ability to capture images of animals on cave walls. And it appears that they hid the artworks to protect them and save them for future generations.

This was creation for creation's sake, in the same way that a modern artist creates beauty and art for the joy of doing it. Yet the "art for its own sake" theory, as well as the shamanistic hypothesis, failed to address the meaning of the signs. The "art for art's sake" theory is actually an early one and predates Tattersall's modern views. According to Leroi-Gourhan, the first scholars to assume that the cave paintings and drawings constitute art for its own sake were Gabriel de Mortillet, Émile Cartailhac, and Edouard Piette in France during the first few years of the twentieth century.

These researchers thought that the art was made by "primitive people" who could not yet have developed the sophistication that would allow them to establish a religion.[11] Leroi-Gourhan attributed to Breuil the idea that "primitive man" goes to a cave to draw a wounded animal as a manifestation of "sympathetic magic."[12] It was this kind of thinking that led to early interpretations of the art as shamanism and eventually to the recent rebirth of this discredited hypothesis through the work of Clottes and Lewis-Williams.

But Clottes and Lewis-Williams's obsession with shamanistic interpretations reaches the point of absurdity when they try to address the mystery of the handprints that cover the walls of the Gargas cave in the Pyrenees. No one knows what the mysterious hands mean, even though many experts have tried to come up with explanations, and Leroi-Gourhan had made some progress in explaining this mystery. Nevertheless, the analysis by Clottes and Lewis-Williams is as follows:

> The negative hand imprints present, from this point of view, something particularly interesting.

In at least one case, at Gargas, the arms of an infant were used in place of those of an adult; in the same cave one finds equally an imprint of a hand of a baby. These representations resemble the customs of the Jivaros and the Inuits where children are incorporated in the shamanistic system. As for other evidence, among the most commented on and the most fascinating we have encountered, confirm that children played a role in Paleolithic shamanism. In a certain number of decorated caves, there were found on the ground footsteps and hands of children.[13]

It seems that this is all that Clottes and Lewis-Williams have to prove their theory. They remark that children are used in present-day shamanistic rituals in Alaska and elsewhere. Then they observe that among the hundreds of handprints at Gargas, two are believed to have been made by the hands of infants. They also note that footprints indicate that children had at certain times entered decorated caves. Clottes and Lewis-Williams then conclude that the children's footprints in some caves and the two infants' handprints at Gargas provide evidence that the purpose of all Paleolithic cave art was shamanistic. It's a good thing scientific work is generally not done this way, or else we would all be in trouble.

In another place in their book, Clottes and Lewis-Williams use one of the most marvelous paintings in the entire Paleolithic period to push their ludicrous theory: the painting of the beautiful pair of dotted horses in Pech Merle, dated to 22,600 years ago.

The artist who created the two horses of Pech Merle was clearly very talented, and he or she (or they) took great pains to achieve a certain artistic effect. This painting overwhelms everyone who sees it. But Clottes and Lewis-Williams seem to have been determined to trivialize it. Here is what they wrote:

> On a larger level, the head of one of the well known "dappled horses" of Pech Merle (Lot) is suggested by the natural cut of the rock, above all when the light is at a certain position. However, in this case, the artist has deformed the head of the painted horse and rendered it ridiculously small. In actuality, the rocky form is much closer to anatomical reality than the painted head. All this passes as if the relief suggested "a horse," but the artist, however, did not paint a "real" horse but a disproportionate horse, perhaps a "spirit-horse"?[14]

Here we find again the persistence of the hypothesis that these were not artists but shamans—and Clottes and Lewis-Williams seem to undervalue the incredible artistic talents of the people who made these great paintings more than two hundred centuries ago.

Leroi-Gourhan himself discredited the earlier version of the shamanistic interpretation when he wrote, "To take what is known about prehistory and cast about for parallels in the life of present-day peoples does not throw light on the behavior of prehistoric man."[15]

Leroi-Gourhan further pointed out that less than 10 percent of the bison drawn, painted, or engraved on cave walls bear what *could be* (but not even certainly so) interpreted as wounds. What, then, was the purpose of the other 90 percent of such images? In fact, of the totality of animals found in decorated caves by the time of Leroi-Gourhan's research, only 4 percent were of wounded animals.[16] He noted that this would imply that the Paleolithic people must have abandoned their project of the hunt in 96 percent of the cases—which he said was absurd. This puts us quite far away from the naive hypothesis that the animals were drawn in caves as a magical way of favoring the hunt. The kinds of depictions of animals and the rarity of wounded animals make it very unlikely that the art of the caves was driven by need.

Furthermore, according to research on the type of animals consumed by Paleolithic people, the reindeer accounts for anywhere from 90 to 98 percent of the meat consumed, depending on the period; while at the same time, the reindeer is only in the seventh position in terms of the frequency of its depictions in cave art—it is a relatively rare animal to be drawn.[17]

What is more likely as an explanation of "wounds" on larger and seldom-eaten animals, according to Leroi-Gourhan, is that what appear to be wounds on the animals are actually signs. He gave the example of a bison in the cave of Bernifal in the Dordogne, which has a vulva drawn on its flank, at the same location on the body where in other caves an arrowhead might appear.[18] We will come back to this idea when I describe Leroi-Gourhan's theory of the signs. It completely destroys any notions about the purpose of cave art being related to the hunt, sympathetic wounds, or shamanism.

Analysis shows that very few images of what might be construed as magicians, sorcerers, or shamans exist on cave walls—a handful, out of thousands of images. Does it make sense to construct a whole theory around so few cases, ignoring everything else in the rich artistic tradition of the Cro-Magnons?

17

Stonehenge and Signs
in the Sky

THE NEW APPROACH BORROWED FROM ANTHROPOLOGY,
that of looking elsewhere on our present-day Earth for hints
about the past in Ice Age Europe, has increased in popularity.
In this vein, one theory about the meaning of cave signs was
recently proposed by Michael Rappenglueck of the University
of Munich. Rappenglueck considered the druids of Stonehenge
and their putative construction of what is widely believed to
have been a stone observatory on Salisbury Plain in England
beginning about five millennia ago. These Neolithic people were
looking for a way to regulate activities by precise determination
of the seasons of the year, and for that, they needed a way to
record time and events. Rappenglueck proposed that the dot
symbols found in the cave of Lascaux are actually the oldest
example of a calendar.

Rappenglueck counted twenty-nine dots around a horse in
the Lascaux cave and has argued that each dot represents a
day in the lunar cycle, hence twenty-nine days. He made other

conjectures about the signs at Lascaux representing the aster-
isms of the Zodiac and other star clusters such as the Pleiades.

According to this theory, the astral knowledge of Lascaux
would seem to have been memorized and later reproduced
in every civilization, as calendars became essential for cyclical
hunting-gathering and finally for agriculture, which arrived from
the Near East some millennia after the end of the Paleolithic.
Rappenglueck first argued that the Magdalenians "needed to
know the lunar cycle and the seasons," perhaps for hunting and
gathering vegetables and berries. Another interpretation was
that the number 29 may have implied a menstrual cycle, and its
importance was in determining pregnancy.

But these theories have been discredited. There are many
dot configurations in European caves, and they only rarely add
up to twenty-nine. Even the original count in the case of one
location within the cave of Lascaux is suspect. There are many
other dots in the surrounding area, and it is not at all clear how
to count them. So where one person might count twenty-nine
dots, others might see thirty or thirty-three or twenty-seven.
Rappenglueck's idea seems to hinge on a comparison between
the most famous prehistoric cave in the world, Lascaux,
and the most well-known stone circle: Stonehenge. Is this
analogy valid?

• • •

My friend Carlo F. Barenghi of the University of Newcastle, my
colleague Timothy Fullam, my wife, and I all took the train from
London heading west to the Salisbury Plain some years ago to
study the riddle of Stonehenge. We got off at Salisbury and traveled by taxi to the nearby village of Berwick St. James. There,
we stayed at a charming country inn called the Mill House, on

a property that included a historic mill on a stream, which was once used to make flour. The next morning, we woke up early and drove up the hill on which Stonehenge is situated. This is certainly one of the most imposing and awe-inspiring prehistoric sites anywhere in the world.

Construction at Stonehenge began around 3100 BC, when a circular bank and ditch were made here by early settlers of the British Isles. This location was wooded at that time, but the actual site was on a patch of grassy knoll. An entrance to the enclosure was made to the northeast and another one to the south. The prehistoric builders used stone tools, some of which have been found in this area. But construction work at Stonehenge continued for thousands of years. Thus, evidence of the use of metals appears after 2000 BC, which marks the beginning of the Bronze Age in Britain.

Step by step, over many centuries, this amazing site changed. Huge stones were brought here in ways that are still not understood by science and were placed in a large circle. Around 2500 BC, the area began to be used in agriculture, and the woods were being cleared by farmers. The stone circle was constructed to align in such a way that the rising sun on the summer solstice day and the setting sun on the day of the winter solstice would appear through the center between the two large stones that make up the northeastern entrance to the circle. A visitor to Stonehenge during the summer solstice, when crowds of "neo-druids" come here to see the sunrise, will easily be convinced that Stonehenge had some astronomical function.

Yet the key point to remember is that this happened during the Neolithic period—after the development of agriculture. At this time, the new farmers certainly needed to understand and fix as precisely as they could the seasons of the year. No such need was evident earlier, and, certainly, there are no obvious alignments by points of the compass around decorated caves.

And the caves are underground. If the Paleolithic people who decorated them so magnificently had been interested in calendars and solstices, wouldn't they have constructed their solar observatories above ground, where the sun can be seen?

Standing near the imposing structure that is Stonehenge, we all felt awed. But I got a very different feeling here from the one I had while visiting many Paleolithic caves. In the caves, one observes a truly ancient art and perceives that it is rich in symbolism and mysterious meanings. At Stonehenge, one is struck by the grandness of the scale: the stones are huge and imposing; they seem to be precisely placed in a circle for a purpose. But the purpose appears to have been different from that of cave art.

What struck us at Stonehenge was the sense of engineering. Here were people who organized a great feat of construction: they hauled stones weighing tons across the terrain and measured and erected them to carry out some engineering plan and to construct something with a physical purpose—most likely, a sun observatory to determine precisely the seasons for agriculture.

• • •

Recently, new research has greatly expanded our understanding of what happened over the millennia at Stonehenge and has shed light on the purpose and function of this imposing and mysterious Neolithic structure.[1]

Stonehenge was built five millennia ago and was among the first major construction projects by Neolithic people. (Another is the Carnac alignment in Brittany.) They learned how to build with gigantic stones using the same methods they had mastered in carpentry: Stonehenge has huge lintels that are bound to the standing stones by mortise and tenon joints.

This was a major undertaking, and for generations people have pondered the meaning of the most famous prehistoric monument in the world. What was it used for? Why did prehistoric people go to an incredible degree of trouble, quarrying and transporting huge blocks of stone that weighed up to thirty-five tons each and placing them upright in a circle, then linking the tops as if they were wooden structures?

Recently, archaeologists have shifted their search for the meaning of Stonehenge from the site itself—which had been studied and analyzed for many decades—to the nearby location of a Neolithic village that existed at that time. Stone circles on circular banks of earth (called *henges*) such as Stonehenge are found in many locations in the British Isles and also in France, but Stonehenge is by far the most famous. The henge itself—a bank of earth surrounded by a ditch—was made around 4,500 years ago, and then the "bluestones" were brought here, probably from Wales. Sometime later, the giant thirty-five-ton Sarsen stones were brought to this location and placed as the outer stone circle linked by lintels. Who were the people who made this colossal monument?

Analyses of fossilized remains of skeletons of the people living in the Neolithic village not far from Stonehenge revealed that these individuals enjoyed overall good health. Their teeth showed little decay, and even though their lives clearly demanded great exertion—this was the beginning of agriculture and the domestication of animals in Britain—their stature seems to have been smaller than that of modern farmers. Surprisingly, however, as much as 6 percent of the population seems to have suffered trauma to the head, which has led some researchers to hypothesize that the community may have practiced some form of "ritualized violence," or that life at this place and time was brutal.[2]

In 2002, archaeologists working in an area only two and a half miles southeast of Stonehenge discovered a burial site and unearthed the remains of a middle-aged man who had a very badly hurt leg, which would have allowed him to walk only with great difficulty. Next to him were found the remains of a younger man, perhaps a son or a relative. The burial ground included gold jewelry and other valuable items of the time. A comprehensive chemical analysis of the teeth of the two men revealed that while the young one was from the area, the older man had come from the Alps, from a region of present-day Switzerland. A British archaeologist, Andrew Fitzpatrick, was able to come up with a plausible story about this man, known affectionately as the Amesbury Archer. The Archer had immigrated to Stonehenge, enjoyed economic success, and had children.[3]

Science is slowly amassing a considerable amount of information about the people who lived in the area of Stonehenge at the time of its construction and who perhaps contributed to that Herculean effort or came from faraway destinations to worship here, admire the monument, or take part in whatever mysterious rites were practiced at this unique place. Evidence has been found showing that before Stonehenge was built, a number of timber circles that resemble it had been constructed in the same area, a mile or two around Stonehenge. The style of these circles made of wooden stakes was very similar, and the carpentry techniques used in their construction was later adapted to this much more massive stone circle.

Archaeologists have also found evidence for a much larger seasonal community living here, which augmented the local population during certain short periods of the year—most likely during the winter and the summer solstices. This may indicate that some kind of ceremony took place regularly at Stonehenge during particular times of the year, and it strengthens the hypothesis—itself supported by the alignment of the stones of this monument—that Stonehenge was a giant astronomical calendar.

Stonehenge may also have functioned as an ancient astronomical observatory. Stars are known to have been very important for people throughout history: both the ancient Egyptians and the Babylonians observed the heavens regularly and recorded their findings, to understand the seasons, as well as for other reasons. But all of this happened after the development of agriculture. And again, research on prehistoric art and signs found in decorated European caves has never led to the definitive identification of any astronomical information. Although many of the signs of the zodiac are animals—and there is certainly a bull featured prominently among them: the constellation of Taurus—the positions of the cave drawings, as well as the existence of many signs, do not seem to correspond to any stars or constellations.

So although Rappenglueck's new theory received much media attention on BBC television programs and elsewhere when he proposed it a few years ago, the hypothesis lacks objective scientific evidence to support it. If one wants to count dots—and there are so many sets of dots in prehistoric caves from which to choose—one can "prove" almost anything. The problem, once again, is that in order to find something meaningful in the cave art and signs, one must always look at the totality of a cave—not merely pick a single piece of art or a single sign— and see which patterns repeat themselves from cave to cave.

There are certainly many caves to explore for patterns, and there are thousands of animal depictions and signs. It is important to adopt some form of statistical reasoning here; otherwise, anyone can claim almost anything. A systematic order must be evident in a majority of locations in order to have statistical and logical significance. Rappenglueck's hypothesis is thus found lacking and explains nothing. The prehistoric artists of Lascaux and elsewhere were not farmers, and they do not seem to have cared about the seasons of the year or to have had any obvious interest in astronomy—at least, not as far as this may objectively be implied by the evidence from cave art.

So, can any other order be discerned in the animal drawings? And is there a uniform theme in the drawings and the signs?

What may be evident as we move from the Paleolithic to the Neolithic is that as human society developed agriculture and domesticated animals, it also gave up the art that characterized the more ancient period: cave drawings and paintings, rock engravings, and the making of mobile art objects. Instead, we see (late in the Neolithic) pottery developed for the purpose of storing and cooking food that was produced by the new agriculture. The pottery may be artistically decorated, but it was created with a specific physical need in mind. Equally, we see large building projects such as Stonehenge, other stone circles, and similar stone constructions, such as the mysterious stones at Hagar Qim, on the southern coast of the island of Malta, which is about the same age as Stonehenge. Neolithic people were interested in architecture—not only monuments, but the first houses were also built during this era—and later in pottery. Their focus was food production, and for that purpose they needed a calendar. This was the end of the old way of life, the Paleolithic with its cave art, and the beginning of a new one with different interests and concerns.

Rappenglueck was not the first person to look for evidence of an ancient calendar in the signs found in Paleolithic caves or the other objects left to us by the Cro-Magnons. In 1964, Alexander Marshack, an independent American scholar, argued that sequences of markings on animal bones found in various shallow Paleolithic caves and rock shelters in France had been arranged in sets of twenty-nine; hence, he inferred that this was a lunar calendar.

There was a problem, however, with Marshack's work. In order to find the markings on the various bones he analyzed, he used a low-power microscope (with magnification power from 10 to 60)—an innovation in the study of prehistoric artifacts. Critics have suggested that such small marks may have occurred by chance, and that in some cases Marshack's counting was wrong.[4] Of course, the big question just begs to be asked: if Marshack had to use a microscope to see the markings on the bones, how did the Paleolithic people who supposedly used them ever read their own markings?

The Russian scientist Boris Frolov conducted a similar analysis (without the use of a microscope) of a plaque bearing complicated markings, which had been found in Malta, Russia, and dated to the Paleolithic. He concluded that this was a calendar of the entire year, showing lunar cycles as well.[5]

The French researcher Jean Pierre Duhard claimed in his doctoral dissertation, published in France in 1989, that the woman with the horn (*Venus with the Horn*) from Laussel had some connection with a baton made of animal bone that was found near the engraving, on which were markings associated with 10.5 lunar months. Similar engraved stones found at Laussel, according to Duhard, represented the number of days in a lunar month. The author then made the connection between the average length of a lunar cycle, 29.5 days, and the average number of days in a menstrual cycle, between 28 and 31 days, and claimed that the lunar cycle was used as a means of counting days from a woman's last menstruation in order to detect a pregnancy. The *Venus with the Horn*, according to him, represents this idea.[6]

It is very difficult to know whether there is anything of value in these theories about counting the markings on bones or stones. Numbers can be arranged in so many possible ways, and there is also the risk that people in search of certain patterns discard or ignore bones or rocks that bear other numbers of markings, leaving them with only the specially selected ones that they think provide evidence for whatever theory they want to prove.

In a sense, this search is similar to the scientifically spurious case of "The Bible Code," which caused a sensation some years ago. There is even a mathematical theorem (Furstenberg's Theorem) that specifies conditions under which any pattern whatsoever can be found in a large-enough collection of possibilities. For example, if you look at the stars on a very clear night outside a region with city lights, you may find stars to fit any preconceived pattern, such as an umbrella, a house, or a boat.

At any rate, regarding the markings on rocks and bones and the signs in Lascaux and in other Paleolithic caves, there is certainly no convincing evidence whatsoever that any kind of calendar was involved here. Lascaux is not Stonehenge.

• • •

Along with Normandy, the other part of France that lies closest to Britain is called Brittany (Bretagne, in French), across the English channel from the British Isles. This region shares a common history with England: it, too, was once settled by Celts, and even today, the houses here, as well as the folk music and the customs, are reminiscent of those in Britain. Large areas of Brittany contain thousands of megalithic (from Greek, "large stone") monuments that were erected by Neolithic peoples living in this region. These monuments resemble Stonehenge, although they are slightly older—the oldest dating from 6,500 years ago—and their arrangement is different. Most Neolithic stone monuments are not circular but are arranged in long, parallel straight lines. They are stunning testaments to the will and the ability of prehistoric people.

What is the meaning of these large constructions? Many scholars have tried to show that the Carnac alignments, on the southern coast of Brittany, bear some astronomical or calendrical meaning: the alignments coincide with the sun's angle during the winter solstice, the summer solstice, or the spring or fall equinoxes. But all of these theories have failed. To date, no one knows what the stone alignments mean. On French soil, therefore, even seven millennia after the last of the cave art was produced, prehistoric people are not known to have constructed calendars.

18

The Mediterranean,
Australia, and Patagonia

OUR UNDERSTANDING OF STONEHENGE HAS CHANGED with new discoveries that reshaped our thinking. But understanding of cave art also changes when we find new artworks. No one would have expected that cave art—which had become familiar to the public through the findings in hundreds of caves—would contain paintings of penguins. Yet this is exactly what turned up in a cave discovered late in the twentieth century.

In 1985, a French recreational diver named Henri Cosquer was exploring the rocky bottom of the Mediterranean near Marseille at a depth of 120 feet, when he suddenly saw what looked like the opening of an underwater cave. Cosquer kept his discovery to himself and over the years explored this cave on his own. There was a narrow entry shaft that extended for more than 360 feet, and every time he went diving in this area, he ventured deeper into the cavity. In 1991, he reached the end of this underwater entryway and emerged into the air of a wide underground hall. On one of its walls, he found the red imprint of a hand. Realizing that he had just discovered a prehistoric drawing, Cosquer reported his finding to the French adminis-trator of antiquities, and a project was launched to explore this cave. But before any official work began there, three divers who had heard about the discovery and came to explore the new underwater cave on their own became trapped there and suf-focated to death. This incident focused world attention on the Cosquer cave, as it became known.

The cave had been eight miles away from the sea during the Ice Age, and its entrance then was on a cliff almost three hundred feet above sea level. The reason for this is that during the Ice Age, much of Earth's water was locked on land or sea in the form of glaciers or icebergs. Since there was much less liquid water around, the level of the world's seas and oceans was lower. When the ice melted, the sea covered the entrance to the Cosquer cave, which was now near the edge of the Mediterranean.

This cave had been entered at least twice during the Paleo-lithic period: once around 27,000 years ago, when its visitors painted the hand that was seen by Cosquer, as well as many other hands later found there; and the second visit by cave art-ists took place at the very beginning of the Magdalenian age, 18,000 years ago. These latter cave artists painted and engraved images of horses, bison, and ibex but also made unique drawings of sea animals: seals and penguins.

During the Ice Age, the Mediterranean was a cold sea (of a smaller size than today), so animals that typically live in the polar regions inhabited this area at that time. Cosquer is the only known cave or location that has Paleolithic drawings of seals and penguins. The cave also contains sexual images, including an engraved penis. In 1991, French archaeologists visited the cave and photographed more than 140 drawings, paintings, and engravings of animals and signs. This strange discovery intensified the mystery of the Cro-Magnon cave art's purpose.

The Mediterranean world was the home of other prehistoric caves as well. As mentioned at the beginning of this book, Paleolithic caves have been discovered in France, Spain, and Italy. The main area of known prehistoric caves is the Franco-Cantabrian region—that is, much of France (but mostly the Dordogne and the Pyrenees regions) and Cantabria, on the Atlantic coast of northwestern Spain. We have therefore ignored the Italian caves until now. They are few, but they belong to the Mediterranean world. These caves are all in southern Italy, on the coast. There are caves in the region of Reggio di Calabria, at the bottom of the Italian "boot," in the regions of Lecce and Matera, and near the Sicilian city of Palermo. The Italian cave art is dated to 14,000 years ago, and some locations have art that is believed to be a few thousand years younger still—thus close to the Neolithic period.

The art in these caves is generally sparser than the abundant art of the Franco-Cantabrian caverns. The most well-known is the Grotta dell'Addaura, on the northeast side of Monte Pellegrino near Palermo, Sicily. This cave has many engravings of horses and bulls, as well as deer. It also has a large panel with strange humanlike figures in various positions, suggesting movement. These have been dubbed "the acrobats," but some scholars believe these figures represent people performing some sort of religious or traditional rite.

· · ·

Paintings and engravings on rocks appear at various locations around the world. And signs, different from those found in European caves, are found on rocks in distant places. But in the

Cueva de las Manos in Patagonia, there are hundreds of imprints of hands that look strikingly similar to the ones found at Gargas and Pech Merle (as well as at Cosquer). The Cueva de las Manos is much younger than the French caves, in terms of human activity, since people arrived here only around 11,000 years ago. Did they bring with them the ideas and techniques of imprinting their hands in deep caves?

There is much Australian aboriginal rock art in Arnhem Land, in the Northern Territory, as well as in other parts of the Australian continent. Decorating rocks was a common pastime of the ancestors of Australia's aboriginal population. Is there a relationship between this art and that of the European caves?

The Cro-Magnons and their ancestors and descendents are known to have dispersed around the world. Modern humans spread into Asia, arriving in Siberia around 35,000 to 25,000 years ago. They crossed the Bering Sea (which was then an icy land area called Beringia) into Alaska about 15,000 years ago and continued down through North America and into South America, arriving in Patagonia 11,000 years ago. Around 4,000 years ago, modern humans began to voyage from Australia and New Guinea into the Pacific Islands, first settling Fiji and Tonga, and arriving in the Marquesas, the Society Islands, and Easter Island only 1,500 years ago. Hawaii was settled 1,400 years ago, and finally New Zealand, 1,000 years before our time.

But the first immigrants to Australia arrived there approximately 50,000 years ago or earlier. Thus, Australian aborigines date back to a time before the Cro-Magnon cultures that decorated the caves of France, Spain, and Italy. What was the aborigines' culture like? Is there anything we can learn from it? And is there a relationship between aboriginal art and that of the Cro-Magnons? Because the aborigines have lived continuously in Australia since the arrival of their ancestors on that continent, we do know something about their traditions.

．． ．

In 2005, I traveled to Australia, hoping to find answers to these questions. My host was a historian of science, Professor Michael Matthews of the University of New South Wales. Michael's wife, Julie House, had spent several years living with an aboriginal tribe in Arnhem Land in northern Australia, and she shared some of her experiences with me.

Australian aborigines have a fascinating, intricate social system that dates perhaps from the Stone Age—according to tradition, it is as old as tribal memory can go back. It is based on complex marriage rules, which have been studied by mathematicians and found to obey certain properties dictated by the abstract theory of groups.[1] These strange rules create complicated social structures and have been a major focus of the research of the eminent French anthropologist Claude Lévi-Strauss.

The marriage rules dictate that a man from one group within a tribe must marry a woman from a specified different group and at the same time is forbidden from marrying a woman from a third group. The groups are defined by family relations— cousins on one side, versus cousins from another side of a family. According to Lévi-Strauss's analysis, the purpose of these rules is both to prevent incest and to form social alliances.[2]

According to Julie House, when one lives with a tribe for some time, one becomes painfully aware of these laws, because they affect everything in the daily lives of the aborigines. Members of a group are not even allowed to look at people belonging to a group that is taboo for them. Everyone within the society knows whom they are allowed to associate with and those who are taboo.

The social structures of the aborigines may well date from their arrival in Australia. The aborigines' stories, traditions, and mythology of the creation of the world originate in what they call Dreamtime. This was the period, millennia ago, when a brother and two sisters—the ancestors of all aboriginal Australians—landed on the northern shores of the continent. They interbred because there was nobody else around. But since then, no one was allowed to marry a sister or a brother. Tribe members are allowed to marry certain cousins, but other cousins are strictly forbidden to them.

This ancient system is clearly designed around the idea of avoiding incest. If other early societies shared this concern, then perhaps Jacques Picard's theory about the scene in the Pit at Lascaux is right, and the allegorical story told there is a warning against incest. But, of course, we must avoid making any comparisons or implications based on living societies. And we should only interpret ideas very cautiously and propose theories that can be scientifically supported.

The ancestors of the aborigines diverged from those of the Cro-Magnons many thousands of years before the first known cave art appeared in Europe. We know this from evidence that the ancestors of the aborigines crossed the land bridge that then existed between Asia and Australia (parts of it were underwater and required passage by boat or raft) about 50,000 years ago or earlier, whereas the oldest European decorated cave is 32,000 years old. But are there any similarities between cave art and aboriginal art?

• • •

After a two-hour flight from Sydney heading toward the very center of the Australian continent, my plane began its descent.

Through the window, I could already see the tall, red, craggy massif rising above the desert floor. This was the famed Ayer's Rock, now referred to mostly by its aboriginal name, Uluru.

We landed on the airstrip just a few miles from the rock, and a bus took me to my accommodations in a rustic makeshift village perched by the side of Uluru. The bed was simple, the room undecorated, and the available food was mostly sandwiches and pizza. Out in the middle of a desert, with the nearest town hundreds of miles away, I was thankful for a sandwich. I packed my small backpack and walked toward Uluru.

It was hot and dry, and the infamous Australian flies headed straight for my eyes, seeking moisture. This made it hard for me to walk, as I swatted my own face while continuing on a lonely road, getting closer and closer to the towering rock. Uluru is considered a holy place by the aborigines, and they try to discourage approach to, or climbing on, this rock. It's a place of the spirits of ancestors. I walked around the mound for some hours. Then I entered the large hut center of aboriginal art.

Here and elsewhere in Australia, I inspected the many paintings and reproductions of art created by the ancestors of today's aborigines. The art is very decorative: there are geometrical designs of many kinds, with repeating zigzag and circular patterns, and these dominate the art of the aborigines. There are paintings of animals and people—but these are all very different from the art of the caves.

The animals and the people show about the same amount of detail, and overall, this level of detail is far less than what we find in the Paleolithic cave art of Europe. There are many rock paintings in northern Australia, but they seem imprecise and dreamlike. In aboriginal art, we don't find the realistic portrayal of animals that is common in European caves. Aboriginal artists do not avoid depicting terrain, and they don't use the technique of overlapping animal figures that we typically find in caves in France and Spain. Aboriginal art is wonderful: it is expressive, decorative, often detailed, and meaningful to its artists and to the popular tribal traditions, which date back so many millennia. But this art does not seem to share much with that of the European caves.

Aboriginal art today is in transition. Australian aborigines have been practicing their unique art on the continent for many thousands of years. In fact, radiocarbon analyses of charcoal from rock paintings in northern Australia have helped scholars date the arrival of anatomically modern humans on the shores of Australia to at least 40,000 years ago (other methods date the arrival to 50,000 years ago). Britain began to colonize the Australian continent intensively around 1788, and waves of immigrants swept over this vast land, completely overwhelming an unprepared native population. With this influx, as well as the resulting worldwide popularity of aboriginal art starting in the 1930s, aboriginal art began to change. The themes depicted in present-day aboriginal art are thus an amalgam of traditional notions and new ideas imported from the outside world.[3]

It is important, therefore, to try to isolate what may be "pure" aboriginal art—that is, art that was produced within traditional milieus of family, tribe, and clan, with as little as possible influence from the outside. Only in this way can we try to effect any meaningful comparison between European cave art and tribal Australian art.

In 1841, Sir George Gray led an expedition to the Kimberley region of Western Australia, where he discovered aboriginal rock paintings. Later in that century, anthropologists joined the search for original art made by Australian natives before the arrival of Western colonists. This culminated in the key work of Ursula McConnel and A. R. Radcliffe-Browne.

The rock paintings at Kimberley are schematic depictions of anthropomorphic beings: they could be people, but they also resemble what some people would describe as "aliens"—oval faces; abstract, almond-shaped eyes; a schematic nose; and a halo over the head. Rock art from Kakadu National Park in Arnhem Land in northern Australia, which is believed to be about 30,000 years old—thus roughly the age of Chauvet cave—looks equally bizarre, abstract, and unreal. These are intricate geometrical designs that remotely resemble imaginary beings. Then, in Koonalda Cave in Northern Australia, strange lines were found that covered an entire cave wall, dated to about 15,000 years ago. What do these rock paintings mean?

Since everything in aboriginal life relates directly to tradition and tribal membership and structure, it is likely that these are depictions of fantastic stories from the Dreamtime oral history of Australia's natives. Australian tribes follow a tradition of symbolism and structure: animals are believed to have souls, and the souls of dead ancestors are present in rocks and hills. The rock art is believed to represent stories from the Dreamtime tradition and perhaps the souls of dead animals or people. At any rate, the art looks decidedly different from that of the European caves.

As interesting as aboriginal art certainly is, my research in Australia reinforced my belief that we should not try to interpret European cave art by what we find in other places on Earth or make comparisons with the customs and the art of living present-day societies. What happened long ago in the caves of Paleolithic Europe was a unique experience that never repeated itself in the history of our planet. This feeling only intensified my quest for the meaning of the mysterious art and signs.

Understanding the meaning of the art and the symbols in Cro-Magnon caves might shed light on more than the Cro-Magnons themselves. It may explain to us something about who we are, how we came here, and where we are going. But an explanation of these drawings, paintings, and signs continued to elude science.

19

Leroi-Gourhan's Theory

INOW WANT TO PRESENT THE ONE THEORY ABOUT European cave art that I believe holds elements of the actual truth about our Cro-Magnon ancestors and the way they viewed their universe.

The French archaeologist and prehistorian André Leroi-Gourhan was born in 1911 and studied at the Sorbonne, where he wrote a dissertation on the archaeology of the north Pacific. He became aware of the prehistory of other regions of the world before addressing his native country's cave art, brought to his attention by his student Annette Laming-Emperaire, whose contributions to his own theories he readily acknowledged in his books. After serving in the French Resistance in World War II, Leroi-Gourhan took up research positions in England, the United States, and Japan. In 1969, having written much about prehistory, he was appointed to the chair held earlier by Henri Breuil at the prestigious Collège de France in Paris.

Leroi-Gourhan attempted the first deep, systematic, and ultimately meaningful analysis of the mystery of cave art and symbols, building on Laming-Emperaire's foundation of fresh, innovative thinking about this old problem. Leroi-Gourhan adopted her insight of not looking at specific paintings or signs in a cave, but rather considering the entire system. This enabled him to achieve concrete results in formulating a theory that I believe comes closest to solving the mystery of cave art.

Generations of researchers have looked at the signs found in prehistoric caves, searching for an alphabet or at least a set of decodable symbols that could convey something meaningful: "Walk fifty steps left and you will find a drawing of a bison," for example. And this is why they all failed. The signs found in these caves are not words in sentences, and they do not combine to give a set of instructions or descriptions.

Leroi-Gourhan surveyed the previously reigning theories about the meaning of the signs in caves and pointed out that all such theories looked at the signs from an "ethnological" point of view of today's societies. Thus, when a wounded animal is depicted (which happens relatively rarely—less than 10 percent of the time), scholars have imputed to this a kind of sympathetic magic. Similarly, the signs, rather than the animals, have been interpreted in a way that reflects today's world. When wide "tectiform" signs were discovered, scholars who believed the magic theories took these signs as further evidence for their hypotheses by assuming that the wide signs were "huts" in which to detain animal spirits.[1] Other signs were seen as magical traps for animals. And there were the usual assumptions about shamanism, where signs were taken to reinforce that theory.

But according to Leroi-Gourhan, these theories suffer from a bias of modern society and the way we view modern-day "primitive" societies. Prehistoric artists had a long history and traditions of their own before they came to their art, and we don't do science justice by imputing to these artists the motives, lifestyles, and thought processes of present-day tribal societies in Africa, Alaska, or Australia.

The interpretation of the signs and their meaning by Leroi-Gourhan proceeds, according to him, in two main directions: first, the connection between the animals depicted in caves and the signs that accompany them; and second, a connection between the signs and sexual symbolism.

He noted that the signs are different from one another in a chronological way: the earliest signs are of a particular, archaic style; later signs show a development of abstraction; and the latest, Magdalenian, signs are yet more abstract. The signs, therefore, can be used as an aid or a method to confirm the dating of cave art.

The most important conclusion Leroi-Gourhan reached was: *"All signs in caves are substitutes for human sexual representations."*[2]

According to Leroi-Gourhan, the systematic consideration of the totality of all signs in all prehistoric caves gives us certitude about this interpretation of the signs. One can clearly see here the progression through intermediary signs over time and can easily track the development of signs from realistic depictions to more and more abstract ones: there is an obvious continuity through time of this increasing abstractness.

Leroi-Gourhan thus made a crucial discovery about the cave signs. The signs belonged to two distinct groups: feminine signs and masculine signs. In early times, the signs were drawn realistically; for example, a sign might be the drawing of a vulva or even of a full female figure. In later periods, the signs were more and more abstract: they were stylized representations of human sexual organs. For example, the sign from the Pech Merle cave that looks like the letter Y was a stylized feminine sign. According to Leroi-Gourhan's strict theory, every sign found in a prehistoric cave in Europe belongs to one of these two groups: male or female. Thus, a sign conveys either the meaning "female" or the meaning "male." Thin signs are male; wide signs are female. The table on page 183 contains signs from caves in France and Spain, each classified according to Leroi-Gourhan as male or female.

Claviform signs are female not because they resemble a vulva but rather because they are an abstraction of the form of a woman's body. The evolution of this sign can be seen in the figure from the cave of Pech Merle, included in the table on page 183. The complete table of all signs found in caves in France and Spain solved the mystery of the signs: every single sign falls into place within one of Leroi-Gourhan's two categories.

Leroi-Gourhan classified the types of signs as follows:

Female Signs:	Male Signs:
Triangles	Barbed signs
Rectangles	Short strokes (*bâtonnets*)
Lattice-shaped signs	Dots
Tectiform signs	
Oval signs	
Claviform signs	
Brace-shaped signs (these are between rectangular and claviform; they simplify the outline of a female figure)	

The kinds of signs vary not only through time but also through space. Thus, there is generally a progression from realistic depictions of sexual organs to signs that are oval, for the female,

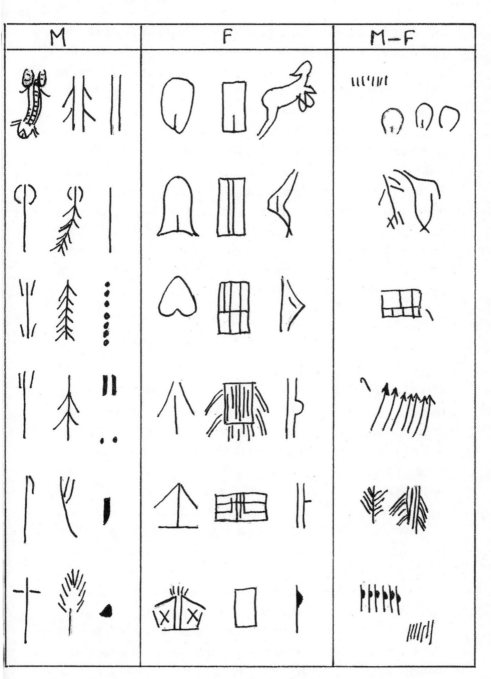

Thomas Barron's signs table.

and long, for the male; then the ovals become more abstract, and, also, signs based on the entire female form become claviforms. But throughout the environment surrounding the cave, there are clear associations as well. For female signs, for example, the region of a few square miles around the town of Les Eyzies-de-Tayac in the Dordogne has caves with an abundance of the tectiform signs. Thus, at Combarelles, Bernifal, Rouffignac, and Font-de-Gaume, one finds many tectiform signs. On the other hand, in caves of the department of Lot, that is, Peche Merle and Cougnac, which lie east of the area of Les Eyzies, there is an abundance of claviform signs. At Pech Merle, which was dated to several periods that spanned thousands of years of artistic work, one finds realistic depictions of the entire female form in its early period of around 20,000 years ago.

• • •

The philosophy of Laming-Emperaire and Leroi-Gourhan was that the decorated cave has a coherent, uniform structure that does not vary across this broad European landscape—from Spain to the French Pyrenees, to the Dordogne, and to Italy—or across the vast span of time: the 20,000 years separating Chauvet from Niaux. Each cave is a complete entity. This very specific structure dictates that each large decorated cave has a side area along which marginal art is displayed. Such art may well have been drawings or studies by novices; it is an area in which the artists practiced.

But the entryway to a typical cave has a very specific structure. There is an "indicative panel" at the entrance to the cave, which has signs on it. The signs found on this first panel as one enters the cave are *masculine* signs, according to Leroi-Gourhan's classification. Here we usually find the following animals: ibex, stags, and sometimes horses. Passages leading out of the entry area repeat that masculine theme, and as one progresses into the cave, there may be depictions of dangerous animals: bears, lions, and rhinoceroses.

There are, at times, some humanlike figures—rough sketches, with no details, of what could be interpreted as human beings. Then there is usually a separating sign, in black or red: perhaps a set of dots or hand signs. This sign indicates the approach to the "deep gallery," in which the principal works of the cave are found.

The number of animals in the cave's main gallery may vary from two to several dozen, and they tend to be larger than in other parts of the cave. Here we find the main theme of the cave. Most frequently, from a statistical point of view, the theme is the coupling of the two main animals: a bison and a horse. Or it could be a very similar coupling: an aurochs (since the aurochs, a type of wild cattle, is similar to a bison) and a horse. Here we also find, in association with the pair or pairs of animals, signs belonging to both categorizations by sex, placed together.

Around the periphery of the main composition of a bovine and a horse, we find the marginal animals that accompany the main composition of the cave. These tend to be ibex or various kinds of deer, but sometimes, as in the case of Pech Merle or Trois Frères, we find humanlike figures in the periphery. There could also be lions here and rhinoceroses.

One of the best examples of the central composition of a decorated cave is the famous ceiling of Altamira. Here, about twenty bison are arranged around the central figure of a horse. Near the largest bison of the group are placed one masculine sign and a set of "claviform" female signs. In the peripheral area around the main animals, there are a female deer, engraved humanlike forms, two boars, and an ibex.

Every cave has this principal theme, which plays out and may repeat itself in various parts of the cave other than the main gallery. At times, a secondary theme—different from the main theme—is represented as well. In a way, this art form is like a symphony, with themes and variations on the themes that repeat themselves throughout the entire composition.

The particular composition that is based on the pairing of an aurochs and a horse is very common and is found at Lascaux, Gabillou, Ebbou, La Passiega in Spain, and in other caves. This theme is often repeated in a different form of the same idea: the bison-horse pair. There are variations of these concepts in different caves. The Pech Merle cave, for example, is characterized by a somewhat different theme. Here we find the predominant motifs of aurochs-mammoth and bison-mammoth. Thus, the mammoth here is the male symbol, and the aurochs and the bison stand for the feminine idea.

The caves of Niaux, Le Portel, Altamira, Castillo in Spain, and Trois Frères, among the principal caves, have the main theme of bison-horse and a secondary motif of aurochs-horse.

According to Leroi-Gourhan, the repetitive patterns one finds in the vast majority of Franco-Cantabrian caves provide strong evidence for his hypothesis that what we are seeing is an underlying ideology of a religious nature.[3] We are unable to truly comprehend the deep essence of this belief system based on the incomplete record provided to us by the cave art discovered thus far. But we can at least grasp something about the underlying philosophy that must have motivated these grand artistic themes so many millennia ago.

Leroi-Gourhan argued that the main concept of animals being associated with sexual symbols repeats itself in mobile art that has also been found outside the Franco-Cantabrian region, in locations that range from Russia and Eastern Europe all the way to the cave of La Pileta near Gibraltar, where mobile art has been found. This is evidence of an ensemble of ancient traditions that perhaps predates Cro-Magnon art itself and that may have matured over millennia before these ideas were expressed in art. These traditions have apparently fed into the entire artistic tradition of Paleolithic Europe.[4]

All art, according to Leroi-Gourhan, follows the trend of being born, maturing, and then disappearing. What is so remarkable about European cave art is that it has absolutely no known antecedents. It simply appeared on the European continent at some point around 32,000 years ago or earlier, and it flourished over millennia before suddenly vanishing without a trace at the end of the Paleolithic period, a few thousand years before the arrival of agriculture in Europe from its origins in the Middle East.

Leroi-Gourhan thought that cave art followed a trajectory that began with a slow start, a great period of fecund creation, during which much of the important cave art was produced, and then experienced a steep decline at the end of the Paleolithic period. France and Spain were "privileged," he wrote, since this was where the artistic activity took place. Although central Europe had its own abundance of natural caves—even deep ones, as in France and Spain—only France and Spain, and to a lesser degree Italy, enjoyed the creation of artworks in deep caves during the Paleolithic era. Many examples of mobile art were found in regions of central Europe as well, but, mysteriously, there was no cave art in these areas at all.

By Leroi-Gourhan's reckoning, the reason for this sudden flowering of art was that small groups of humans living in communities across the entire European continent, from Russia to the Iberian Peninsula, grew and forged connections among themselves, which allowed for the flow and maturing of ideas, which then led to the appearance of both mobile and parietal art.

The figures on cave walls and objects of art demonstrate the existence of ideas that have had time to mature over many thousands of years. As evidenced by the cave signs, these ideas slowly gave rise to styles and symbols with regional nuances that nevertheless still expressed the main philosophical concepts in the lavish art. To this end, Leroi-Gourhan brought up the existence of "marginal" schools of this art on the Mediterranean coast, as evidenced by certain caves there, as well as in Sicily. But the main themes are the most important element here and not the regional variations. These, according to Leroi-Gourhan, exhibit the hallmark of a religion that developed in Paleolithic Europe and then disappeared without a trace.[5]

At the entrance to the cave one finds male signs. Then around the main composition of the cave one finds the female signs. Often, male signs accompany female signs. This can be seen in the following image, which shows four pairs of M-F signs:

The position of the signs in the caves indicates an association: female-bison (also female-aurochs) and male-horse. This is what appears statistically in the majority of the cases in Paleolithic cave art. During the greatest part of the period when prehistoric cave art was produced, the subject matter and the execution of artworks on cave walls followed a predetermined order, a well-planned scheme, although just what that scheme was remains a mystery. We can, however, glimpse parts of it: the sexual associations between animals and genders, the sexual symbolism of the signs, and the general structure of a decorated cave. The central theme seems to be of a binary opposition and of the complementary nature of male and female values.

In Paleolithic art, this particular representation doesn't concern only sexual attributes, but also seems to involve an artificial division of the animal world into creatures associated somehow with a male character and those of a female character.[6]

Then, as one approaches the deeper part of the cave, one finds panels of signs. In the past, these signs were called indicative panels, because earlier researchers took them for coded descriptions of the art to follow or as other types of indications. But Leroi-Gourhan thought otherwise. The indicative panels of signs were part and parcel of the art to come. The panels were aligned in a uniform way that did not vary from cave to cave or through the passage of time: they pointed to the way out of the cave, as well as to the "sanctuary"—the deepest hall within the cave.

The main art within each cave was found in the deepest, most hidden part of the cave. And here, a hierarchy existed. But to understand that hierarchy and how it relates to the signs within the sanctuary and on the panels outside, one had to know what the Cro-Magnon artists saw in the animals.

Leroi-Gourhan discovered a rule by which male signs are placed on the indicative panel of a cave and are then followed by female signs in the depths of the cave and especially in the "deep gallery." In some cases, there are also mixed male and female signs inside the cave. An exception to this rule is the cave of Cougnac, in the French department of Lot.

The cave of Cougnac is in many ways a sister to the cave of Pech Merle, located about twenty-five miles away to the southeast. Both caves have strange humanlike figures. But Cougnac is an unusual cave, even in the way it was discovered. This was the only cave to be found via divination. In 1949, a dowser named Fernand Lagarde pinpointed on an area map the location in which he said there should be a large underground cave. An excavation party was sent there and indeed discovered the cave.

At Cougnac, there is an indicative panel at the front of the cave with male signs, and as one moves farther into the cave, one finds the main composition of this cave: deer, mammoth, ibex, and stag. There are some brace signs (interpreted by Leroi-Gourhan as female) and an outline of a man pierced by arrows.

This is atypical, and this cave does not have the usual horse-bovine pairing. But the cave is incomplete. There are indications that it is part of a vast underground network, the art of which has not yet been discovered. It is quite possible, therefore, that the animals mentioned previously are simply the usual accompanying animals and that the main composition, along with the signs usually associated with it, will be found someday in the depths of this cave.

Cave art was, according to Leroi-Gourhan, an economic oddity. Here was an activity that demanded much from the people who took part in it—in material, time, and effort—and yet there was no apparent economic benefit from this artistic production for the groups of people who practiced it. This anomaly led Leroi-Gourhan to consider that perhaps the art played a religious role in the life of the community.

He started from the notion that there are three main explanations for the purpose of the cave art: "art for art's sake," magical art, and, finally, religious art. He understood that the animals themselves were symbols. The way the animals were displayed on the cave walls was never random, as some had previously assumed, but rather followed specific rules. The two main animals in the cave drawings and paintings were the bison and the horse. Other animals—felines, bears, mammoths, ibex, deer, and fish—were all accompanying secondary figures.

This relationship was a statistical one and needed data to support it. As Leroi-Gourhan analyzed thousands of cave paintings and drawings from France, Spain, and Italy, it became clear to him that there was a duality in the art: a bison was always

accompanied by a horse at some location on the cave wall—
either next to it or on a facing wall.

Sometimes this coupling was easily discerned, and at other
times one had to look around—but it was always there. In some
cases, the secondary animals intervened and masked this pattern, but once you knew what to look for, you could always
find it. In certain instances, the coupling was achieved in a
sophisticated way. For example, a male horse might be drawn
next to a female bison, both surrounded by mammoths and deer,
and on an adjacent wall would be found a male bison next to a
female horse.

This insight—Leroi-Gourhan's breaking of the code of the
animal drawings and paintings—generated enormous excitement
in the scientific community. For the first time in decades, someone had found a real effect, discerned a real pattern in the vast
majority of the works of art in European caves. But what was the
meaning of this coupling of horse and bison? And what was
the relationship between the animals and the signs? A hint
was found in a bison from the cave of Bernifal in the Périgord.
This bison not only had an arrow drawn on its back, it was also
decorated with the drawing of a vulva.

20

The Relationship between Signs and Animals

WHAT IS THE RELATIONSHIP BETWEEN THE SIGNS AND the animals? According to Leroi-Gourhan, the animals themselves are directly related to the sexual signs. The bison, for example, was viewed as female, while the horse was viewed as a male symbol. Therefore, the bison is most often accompanied by the female signs—arrows, drawings of vulvas, oval signs, tectiforms, claviforms—while the horse is accompanied by male signs: sets of points, lines, and thin batons. The secondary animals may convey gender symbolism as well and are often accompanied by signs of one gender or another, but they play a subservient role to those of the animals conveying the main message of the cave art.

The overall message of cave art, or perhaps the religion it symbolizes, is that of opposites in nature and life: the world is divided into two types, two kinds of things, two genders. There is light and darkness, life and death, success and failure, love and hate, the bison and the horse, and, most important of all, male and female. If cave art conveyed the belief of a people akin to a religion, this religion was perhaps similar to the Eastern yang and yin—male and female signs, forever intertwined.

According to Leroi-Gourhan, the duration of time that the decorated caves were frequented has a religious significance. Some of the grottos, such as Lascaux, were used only during a single period. Other caves, such as Altamira or Font-de-Gaume (and Chauvet, of which he couldn't know), had very long periods of being frequented by people—thousands of years from the first entry to their abandonment. Here we see that each period brought its own style of art. This led Leroi-Gourhan to hypothesize an analogy between the Paleolithic decorated caves and modern churches.

He divided the depictions found inside a decorated cave into three categories: animals, human beings, and signs. Leroi-Gourhan counted each panel on a cave wall or ceiling as one "subject," based on the key animal in the ensemble of elements on the particular panel. Thus, he had a "bison subject," an "ibex subject," or a "human subject." Using these characterizations, he conducted a statistical analysis of 1,794 subject panels and obtained the following breakdown (this includes mobile art as well):[1]

Subject of Panel	Percentage of Total (%)
Horse	24
Signs	15
Bison	15
Ibex	7
Reindeer	6.5
Aurochs	5
Deer	4.5
Human	4
All other	19

He noted that a full 54 percent of all motifs are the bison, the horse, or the signs. Other figures intervene only in secondary roles. He then offered two possible explanations: either the bison and the horse were the main food animals and thus appeared frequently, or we have here a kind of mythology based predominantly on the motif of bison-horse signs. Leroi-Gourhan aimed to prove that the second hypothesis was the correct one.[2]

The people of the Paleolithic ate mostly reindeer, ibex, fish, and other small animals. The bison and the horse—based on analyses of bones found in dwelling caves—were never a serious food source for the Cro-Magnons.

Leroi-Gourhan presented a breakdown of the signs. He demonstrated how male signs are sometimes coupled with female signs. He also made a crucial observation: that depicted animals rarely show sexual characteristics, such as the sex organs, while the people represented on cave walls or in mobile art are most often portrayed with their sexual organs and frequently are reduced to these organs. His conclusion was that both the animals and the signs are symbols, and these symbols are based on human sexuality. He divided the animals into four categories and the signs into three categories:

Animals	Category	Signs	Category
Horse	A	Thin	M
Bison	B	Wide	F
Aurochs	B	Special	N
Stag, mammoth, ibex, reindeer	C		
Bear, feline, rhinoceros	D		

Leroi-Gourhan claimed that the distribution of animals and signs in the various areas of a typical decorated cave are not random. The horse appears in the center and the margins of the main composition; the bovines (aurochs or bison), in 90 percent of the cases, appear in the most clear, open, and central locations. The signs of type F turn up on 80 percent of the panels (above all, at the perimeter and in the diverticulum). Only in a small percentage of the cases are animals of class C located in a central position in the cave, and they characteristically peak in percentages in the perimeter. The stag statistically tends to be in the depths of the cave. Animals of class D also appear in the depths of the cave (this, incidentally, is confirmed by Chauvet).

Leroi-Gourhan claimed that although it may be difficult to interpret the meaning of these arrangements, their consistency from cave to cave and period to period is not in question. It is clear that the bison and the aurochs play a central role in 70 percent of the grottos he studied. In only three decorated caves are both of these animals absent. And in 90 percent of the cases, these animals occupy the best panels of the cave—that is, in the sanctuary or the main gallery of the cave. It is also evident that the horse is always present where a bovine is shown, which makes us understand that this is the most significant pair.

The signs of type M and F are situated close to the horse and the bison, and Leroi-Gourhan noted that 90 percent of the F signs are in the center of the cave: prime locations. These are feminine signs, and they are often found in the diverticula as well. Often, they appear together as a group, such as in the cave of La Pasiega.

The mammoth presents some problems of location. In the caves located in the area of Les Eyzies, that is, at Combarelles, Font-de-Gaume, Bernifal, and Rouffignac, the mammoth invades the usual art space all the way in to the central panels, even though it's an animal of group C, which means it should be peripheral. At Pech Merle, however, it is in the periphery.[3]

In general, animals of group C are confined to the periphery, and those of group D are found in the deepest reaches of the cave—beyond the main galleries. The frequency that group D animals appear in the inner depths was first noted by Abbé Henri Breuil, who remarked that the felines, the rhinoceroses, and the human figures are found in the far reaches of the caves. Except for the human figures, these are group D animals, and to them Leroi-Gourhan added the bear. Of the group C animals, the stag may also be found in the inner reaches of the cave.

It should be pointed out that all group C animals may also be found in the inner depths, as happens clearly in Rouffignac; ibex and mammoths are in the very inner part of the cave. Human figures, according to Leroi-Gourhan, are the element with the highest presence in the inner depths of the caves, with 57 percent presence there.

He also hypothesized that the hands that appear in many caves are substitutes for signs. According to Leroi-Gourhan, small handprints, which he takes to be feminine, are often found in locations where a female sign might be found in other caves. In the cave of Pech Merle, he noted, signs of the M kind (male) are paired with small handprints. This is another form, according to Leroi-Gourhan, of matching female and male signs as found elsewhere. In the cave of Gargas, where there are more than a hundred handprints, he hypothesized that the handprints, male and female, stand for the animals of both kinds.[4]

According to Leroi-Gourhan, the coupling of the animals is evident everywhere in the decorated caves. An animal of group B (a bison or an aurochs) will practically always be found opposite a horse (group A). The central theme of Paleolithic art is decidedly, then, a binary motif associating a horse with a bison or with a wild bull. Exactly the same idea is reflected in the signs, with signs of type M and F being coupled.[5]

The coupling of animals or signs may be sophisticated, rather than simple. In caves that contain a lot of complicated art, one may find male or female bison coupled with horses and mares, and at times the coupling is even more complex: sometimes there may be several small horses paired with a large wild bull or bison. In the rotunda of Lascaux, for example, a line of wild bulls (aurochs) is found facing a single male horse. Some tens of feet away, in the diverticulum (the axial gallery), we find a wild cow (a female aurochs) surrounded by little horses and turned toward a feminine sign, which itself is facing the next panel on which there is a large black bull in front of a horse and a masculine sign. The variations can diverge even further. We have seen the coupling of animals and signs, and the pairings of couples. But it is also possible to have a dominant aurochs with a complementary bison, or a dominant bison and a complementary aurochs facing a horse or several horses.

The proportions of the animals of each species vary in a way that may have some significance. Then these primary animals of groups A and B, coupled in intricate ways and often paired with male and female signs, are supported in the periphery by animals of groups C and D.

At Niaux, for example, on Panel 3 we find a large bison accompanied by a small horse, a large horse is flanked by a small bison, and a small ibex completes the scene. Then there is a large ibex above a small horse and a small bison. At Rouffignac, in the engraved ensemble of animals, we find a horse and a bison in the center, surrounded by a troupe of mammoths.

At Pech Merle, the first part of the black fresco has a group of aurochs and horses with two mammoths at the border of the panel; then there is a group made up of bison and horses surrounded by a half-dozen mammoths. Many such examples occur in France, Spain, and southern Italy, so that this symbolic structure in Paleolithic caves should be obvious to anyone who studies them.[6]

Leroi-Gourhan made a fundamental discovery about structure and has come the closest, perhaps, to decoding the mystery of the art of the caves. Furthermore, in his opinion, what is evident in Paleolithic caves is a mythology and perhaps even a fundamental kind of religion based on pairing male and female symbols.

• • •

Leroi-Gourhan imagined a traveler from outer space who might come to Earth and observe churches and cathedrals. Such a visitor would try to gain knowledge about these buildings by looking at as many churches as he could and trying to draw an inference about what their purpose was. What are these cathedrals? Why were they built? What goes on inside them? He noted that the interstellar visitor would quickly see that there are many different kinds of churches, basilicas, and cathedrals, but he would find some common elements in all of them, which would allow him to attempt to infer answers to the above questions.

An interstellar traveler who visited decorated Paleolithic caves would face a similar situation. Based on the previous discussion about the structure of a cave (which was a prehistoric cathedral, according to Leroi-Gourhan), the traveler would reach certain conclusions: the caves are organized spatially following a system that reflects a degree of metaphysical thinking. Signs of type M and animals of group A are linked together, and signs of type F and animals of group B are linked. Sometimes, the signs are replaced by figures of women and men (M by male figures and F by female ones).

The animals of groups C and D and most human depictions occupy intervals between main panels in the typical cave. Often, they also appear in the inner recesses beyond the main galleries.

Working with incomplete information, Leroi-Gourhan divided parietal and mobile art in Europe into styles he numbered from I to IV, in what he thought was a chronological fashion.

The styles of cave paintings, signs, and mobile art change, according to his interpretation, from less detailed in the more ancient period (Aurignacian) to more detailed as one moves forward in time, to finally arrive at the Magdalenian period. But this understanding was revised in 1994, when the Chauvet cave was discovered in the Ardèche region of France. Here was a very ancient cave, dated to as early as 32,000 years ago—it is, in fact, the most ancient cave ever discovered—and yet the art in it is very detailed and modern looking. Chauvet, in many ways, is one of the greatest caves ever discovered.

It should be noted that there are alternative views to those of Leroi-Gourhan. A large book published by the Group for Reflection on Prehistoric Parietal Art (see Aujoulat, et al., in the reference section) follows a different approach to cave paintings and drawings. The group, composed of a number of contemporary French experts on Paleolithic art, including Jean Clottes, concentrates in its treatise on purely descriptive or taxonomic approaches to parietal art. This means that the group members are interested only in describing in detail all elements of Paleolithic art without any (or, rather, with very little) interpretation of the meaning of this great art.

The book is a collection of essays by its editors and authors. An essay in this collection by Georges Sauvet aims to analyze the signs found in Paleolithic caves in France and Spain. Sauvet started by surveying Leroi-Gourhan's classification of signs into male and female.

He then offered his alternative view, which is purely descriptive rather than interpretative. Sauvet broke down the totality of signs found in prehistoric decorated caves into derivations of simple geometry. He listed all signs derived from the idea of, respectively, a square, a circle, an oval, a triangle, a point, and a line.

Although it is hard to argue against the notion that a given sign may have been derived from a circle or a square, one wonders what the value is of such a simple analysis that has no aim beyond a mere description. What interpretative hypotheses do we put forward and test, based on this classification? What inference can we draw from the fact that a given sign resembles a triangle?

Essentially, this is the difference between other experts and Leroi-Gourhan and Annette Laming-Emperaire: they could see beyond a simple classification and tabulation. The latter were looking for the why and not simply the how of Paleolithic cave art and signs. They tried to see beyond the obvious and to glimpse some truth about the purpose of the art and the signs. But they were followed by a generation of French taxonomists who had little vision or perception. It is unfortunate that no expert has come forth who could further pursue the great work begun by these two intellectual giants of French prehistory.

Another opposing view emerged in 1975, when a British scientist, Anthony Stevens, used a computer to attempt a comprehensive statistical analysis of all aspects of cave art known by that time. The main idea was to compare the art content of one cave with the next, rather than simply looking at the prevalence of horses and bison, as in Leroi-Gourhan's analysis.

The study examined thirty-seven caves—itself a small number, from a statistical point of view. Many other caves were excluded because they contained what Stevens thought were too few paintings or engravings. The analysis found that the three main Spanish caves of Altamira, La Pasiega, and El Castillo were similar in the proportions of various animals they contained, while a similarity also existed among the caves of Marsoulas, Montespan, Niaux, and Le Portel—all of which are in the Pyrenees region.[7] Another cluster was the caves of the Dordogne, and geographical similarities were also recognized elsewhere.

This phenomenon is not surprising, and, of course, one would expect that caves found in close proximity would, in general, be similar. Actually, without doing any computer work, anyone visiting the caves of Pech Merle and Cougnac comes away with the understanding that these caves were decorated by artists who had some relationships with one another, who had exchanged ideas, or who were in fact the same people.

The computer analysis did not counter the findings of Leroi-Gourhan. It is difficult to fault his main discoveries, although others have argued that his concentration on sexual symbolism may have injected his own modern ideas into Paleolithic cave art.[8] On the other hand, when one sees the predominance of clearly sexual images in caves such as Chauvet, one is strongly inclined to believe Leroi-Gourhan's interpretation, which he arrived at long before Chauvet was discovered.

The first serious challenge to Leroi-Gourhan's theory came in 1967, in a book by Peter Ucko and Andrée Rosenfeld, which contained a scathing attack on all of Leroi-Gourhan's ideas. Their book had a devastating effect on cave art scholarship: it put an end to deep speculations about the purpose of cave art, for the most part, resulting in the current descriptive approach to the topic, which lacks profound interpretations.

Their arguments are as follows. First, Ucko and Rosenfeld take issue with Leroi-Gourhan's definition of the parts of a cave. They argue that all caves are different, and hence there is no "typical cave" about which people can draw inferences. Arguments of topography, according to the two authors, are completely unreliable.[9] Anyone who has visited a decorated cave knows, however, that this is not a very strong argument. Most caves have a definite structure with a corridor leading to a natural large hall, in which—clearly by design—most of the important art is placed. So to argue that there really is no structure to caves is simply wrong.

Next, Ucko and Rosenfeld claim that Leroi-Gourhan did not consider in his analysis the size of the animals. Thus, if a stag was large and a bull was small, and there was a horse in the same panel, he decided to pair the horse with the small bison, rather than with the large (and perhaps, according to them, more important) stag.[10] They criticized Leroi-Gourhan for not considering the element of color in the displays, although it is not clear what this would do to change his analysis, and they take issue with his choice of the coupling of animals. Leroi-Gourhan considered only whole panels, rather than individual depictions of animals—which is a mainstay of his analysis and which stemmed from Laming-Emperaire's work—and Ucko and Rosenfeld take issue with this practice, saying it may have masked other relationships.

They disapprove of the fact that Leroi-Gourhan did not consider the number of animals in a coupling: thus, when there is a display of several bison, as in Altamira, and they appear together with a horse, Leroi-Gourhan considers this panel to be a coupling of a horse with a bison. Ucko and Rosenfeld disagree—they seem to demand that a couple consist of two animals only, regardless of the panel.

They are also critical of the criteria Leroi-Gourhan chose to define the separations among groups of animals—where does one group end and another begin? They wrote, "Leroi-Gourhan is very free in his handling of spatial separation of representations and this fluidity may well be connected with his view that 'coupling' is fundamental to Paleolithic parietal art although juxtaposition, completion, and framing also play a part in Paleolithic artistic organization."[11]

These authors disagree with Leroi-Gourhan's use of statistics. The essence of their criticism is aimed at the observation, assumed both by Leroi-Gourhan and earlier by Laming-Emperaire, that the horse is most often coupled with a bovine. By separating bovine into bison and aurochs, these authors are able, of course, to lower the persuasive statistical power of Leroi-Gourhan's argument. They wrote, "How far this numerical evidence for 'associations' really indicates conscious grouping and not a haphazard distribution is not easy to assess."[12]

Ucko and Rosenfeld are critical of Leroi-Gourhan's study of the signs in caves, saying, "It cannot be assumed that just because triangles (with base either at top or bottom and with a vertical line within it) appear to some modern eyes to resemble vulvas that they did also to Paleolithic man. Furthermore, many of the stylized signs classed by Leroi-Gourhan as derivations from the 'naturalistic' representation of vulvas or female bodies are extremely difficult to accept."[13]

But what Ucko and Rosenfeld seem to have forgotten was that Leroi-Gourhan did not make his assertion about the symbolism of the signs found in caves in a vacuum. There has been a very rich context to his discovery, based on the fact that in addition to the art found in deep caverns, there was also surface art: mobile statuettes (mostly feminine and emphasizing sexual organs) and, more important, rock engravings.

These have been dated to the same period as the cave art and are found in the region of the caves. In particular, hundreds of rock engravings of vulvas—some very naturalistic in appearance and leaving no doubt about their meaning, and others slightly more stylized but still quite clearly denoting female anatomy—have been found in the region around Les Eyzies in the Dordogne. The actual locations of finds in this area were Blanchard, Castanet, Cellier, La Ferrassie, the Abri Poisson, Pataud, and Laugerie-Haute.

Rocks bearing multiple engravings of vulvas have also been found inside caves, such as the caves of Cavaille (one of the largest such engravings), Comarque, Cazelle (a dozen aligned representations), Saint-Cirq, Fronsac, and Combarelles, all in the Dordogne.[14] From these realistic or somewhat stylized representations of vulvas to the more symbolic ones in signs in caves, the distance is not at all great. It is difficult to question Leroi-Gourhan's assertion with any conviction.

But Ucko and Rosenfeld are not convinced, and they end their book by asking, "Is there anything definitely known about Paleolithic man's reasons for painting, engraving, and sculpting on rock walls? The truthful answer is: very little indeed."[15]

They continue by saying that even though Australian aboriginal artists are alive today and can be asked about the meaning of their art, much is still not known about it—all the more reason that we should not think we understand anything about art created so many millennia ago.

These were certainly biting condemnations of Leroi-Gourhan's theories, and the authors provided none of their own, saying instead that we don't know and may very well never know anything about the purpose of Paleolithic cave art. Ucko and Rosenfeld seem to have undertaken a project of destroying hypotheses without offering a scientific alternative. And one could well argue that the criticism was unfair.

At any rate, the true test of any scientific theory is its ability to predict new observations, those that were unavailable when the theory was formulated. And here, Leroi-Gourhan's theory performed marvelously well, because long after his theory was proposed and long after these criticisms were made, the cave of Chauvet was discovered in the French Ardèche in 1994. And what was found there provided a glorious confirmation of Leroi-Gourhan's ideas.

21

The Chauvet Cave

ANDRÉ LEROI-GOURHAN'S THEORY DID NOT EXPLAIN THE meaning of every painting, and there were occasional exceptions to the rules he deduced. But forty years after he first proposed his theory, it is the one conjecture that still enjoys strong statistical and scientific support from the evidence found in caves.

A decade after Leroi-Gourhan died, in 1994, the Chauvet cave was discovered in the region of the Ardèche in France. As mentioned earlier, this cave contained the oldest art ever discovered—dating from 32,000 years ago. And the signs found in this cave supported Leroi-Gourhan's theory very well. The signs were very explicit drawings of vulvas, and they illustrated how the later stylized depictions had been derived from them during the following millennia.

The "sorcerer" found at this cave was actually a bison superimposed on a realistic drawing of the lower part of a woman's body, including the legs, the pubic triangle, and the vulva—thus reinforcing Leroi-Gourhan's assertion that the bison symbolized a female figure. Plate 16 is a drawing by the artist Thomas

Barron of the image called *The Sorcerer*, which is found at the very end of the cave of Chauvet.[1]

Plate 16. The composite image of *The Sorcerer* from the End Chamber at Chauvet cave, drawn by the artist Thomas Barron.

It took an artist to give one of the best descriptions of this enigmatic piece, which French scholars have assumed was a kind of sorcerer, part human and part bison. According to Barron, the Cro-Magnons were having fun with shapes. They thought the strange-formed rock on which they made their drawing resembled a pubic triangle, so they drew one above it, along with the rest of the lower part of the woman. Then they added the bison, whose head resembled the pubic triangle tilted to its side. This was their "visual pun," according to this modern artist.

The Chauvet cave, with its carnivores and herbivores, large animals paired with small ones, hunting lions opposite grazing mammoths, and at its center a bison and a horse, clearly confirmed Leroi-Gourhan's deciphered message of the prehistoric Cro-Magnons: we live in a world of opposites. Our universe is divided into male and female, and the harmony of nature is ensured by opposites.

•   •   •

The Chauvet cave is located on a bluff overlooking a meandering section of the Ardèche River in eastern France near a place called Pont d'Arc. Chauvet has been extensively radiocarbon dated, and there is evidence that humans visited this cave during two periods. The first group were Aurignacians, and the radiocarbon dates for their presence in the cave span from approximately 32,900 years before the present to about 29,670 years ago. The second period of occupation of the cave by humans was from approximately 26,980 years before the present to about 24,770 years before our time.

So we can say that humans visited the cave around 30,000 years ago or earlier and then again around 25,000 years ago. This is the earliest known cave art, because most of the important artworks here are from a period as far back as 32,000 years ago. The cave has the following parts:

The (entrance) Chamber of Bear Hollows
The Morel Chamber
The Brunel Chamber
The Cactus Gallery
The Red Panels Gallery
The Rouzaud Chamber
The Candle Gallery
The Hillaire Chamber
The Skull Chamber
The Gallery of the Crosshatchings
The Horse Sector
The Megaloceros Gallery
The End Chamber

As we enter the Brunel Chamber, we see a clear claviform sign—a female sign, by Leroi-Gourhan's classification. Then we notice an array of wide dots, palm prints without the fingers. This is an indicative panel that leads farther into the cave. As we continue along, we encounter sketches of animals drawn on the walls: rhinoceros, bear, and ibex. There is little detail here; these are simply red outlines of animals. Farther in, there is a large, wide tectiform sign—which is female, by Leroi-Gourhan's system.

In the *Panel of Handprints*, we find two hands in red, a semicircle of dots, and a bear's head. On the same panel, we see several red rhinoceros drawings and a W symbol, which would be female by Leroi-Gourhan's system, if the symbol had been known in his days—but this discovery came later. We could still interpret it as a wide sign that is therefore female. In the Horse Sector, several horses are surrounded by reindeer. There is a beautiful drawing in black of two fighting rhinoceroses. The theme here seems to be rhinoceroses, horses, and reindeer.

When we enter the Megaloceros Gallery, we encounter the bison accompanied by an ibex. Then we reach the End Chamber, which is the most glorious part of the cave of Chauvet. Here all of the animals are drawn in amazing harmony. On the left panel is a group of three hunting lions, which seem to be in motion, their mouths open as if smiling—they almost look human. Behind them are four rhinoceroses, which also appear to move in the same direction, left, with the hunting Lions.

Farther to the right and into the recess at the end of the cave is a large charging bison, accompanied by two majestic mammoths and four bison. Then there are bears, a bison, and seven more lions in motion—all facing the same direction, left. Far to the right side are two large bison—larger than the other animals. One is standing straight, and the other (dubbed *The Sorcerer*) is bending down and has a humanlike front paw. Below him is the bottom part of a woman, with a pubic triangle and a vulva, as well as the legs.[2]

The End Chamber is, of course, the "deep gallery" of this cave, the location of the most extensive, most detailed, most precious art inside the cave of Chauvet. Besides the female lower body that is directly associated with the bison, Chauvet is rife with actual, naturalistic drawings of human vulvas. These stand alone without any other anatomical body parts. The Megaloceros Gallery has four drawings of vulvas, two of them with pubic triangles.

What we see, therefore, are the very beginnings of the cave language of the Cro-Magnons. The Aurignacians who decorated the cave of Chauvet more than 30,000 years ago exhibited associations of animals. The animals drawn here are different from the most commonly drawn animals of the Magdalenian or Solutrean times. (There are no paintings in Chauvet; the cave has only drawings in red or black, or engravings, as well as signs in these two colors or engraved on the cave walls.) Chauvet artists preferred large, "dangerous" animals: lions, rhinoceroses, and mammoths.

But the cave of Chauvet also features the symbolism of the usual animal pair: horse and bison. These two animals are still prevalent, even in this very ancient cave. And we see here the very genesis of Leroi-Gourhan's sexual symbolism. The female sign is an actual realistic drawing of the vulva, and it is associated with the bison in at least one important case: the image dubbed *The Sorcerer*.

So the early cave of Chauvet gives us strong evidence for Leroi-Gourhan's theory, obtained a decade after his death. His theory is perhaps the best tool we have for opening up the mystery of the cave art and signs to future analysis.

Like the scene of the pit at Lascaux, the shocking depiction of a bison superimposed on the lower part of a woman's body—in itself highly unusual because it is the only detailed human figure, alas incomplete—has stunned and intrigued the world of Paleolithic art research. As in the case of the Lascaux pit scene, *The Sorcerer* has spawned theories about its meaning. It does reinforce several of Leroi-Gourhan's hypotheses about the bull and the feminine symbol, as well as about the signs that developed from the realistic depiction of a vulva.

But the most interesting theory about the meaning of this strange composite image was put forward by the French prehistorian Claudine Cohen. Ms. Cohen began her intriguing book *La femme des origins* (The woman of origins), which is about the images of woman through prehistory, with a description of *The Sorcerer* of Chauvet. She ended the description of the lower part of a woman's body superimposed below the head and the neck of a bison by saying, "Such is the woman of our origins, the most ancient of all, recently discovered in the cave of Chauvet near Avignon. Thirty thousand years before Courbet, a prehistoric artist painted and engraved in a bend on a rock the sex of a woman—the origin of the world."[3]

Cohen placed the most ancient depiction of a woman from the Chauvet cave within the context of the many female statuettes that are found all over Europe, dated roughly 22,000 to 17,000 years ago. What are these "Venus figurines," as they have been called? Are they fertility goddesses? Are they symbols? Or was this a female archetype, always embedded in human consciousness since time immemorial, which is why she was depicted by an ancient artist?

Carl Jung, the pioneer of modern psychology, wrote about the *Venus of Willendorf* in describing and analyzing a dream: "The personal association that Henry contributed to the prostitute was the 'Venus of Willendorf,' a little carved figure (from the Paleolithic age) of a fleshy woman, probably a nature or fertility goddess."[4]

Within the same dream sequence, the psychoanalytic patient called Henry also described caves, which Jung interpreted as follows:

> Moreover, rock caves may be symbols of the womb of Mother Earth, appearing as mysterious caverns in which transformation and rebirth can come about. Thus the dream seems to represent Henry's introverted withdrawal—when the world becomes too difficult for him—into a "cave" within his subconscious where he can succumb

to subjective fantasies. This interpretation would also explain why he sees the female figure—a replica of some of the inner feminine traits of his psyche. She is the formless, spongy, half-hidden prostitute representing the repressed image in his unconscious of a woman who Henry would have never approached in conscious life.[5]

So, who is the *Venus of Willendorf*, a symbol of femininity? Of fertility? Of motherhood? Or of wantonness? Perhaps all of them or none at all, but rather something we may never understand. One way or another, she is a primeval symbol embedded in our collective human consciousness. And perhaps so is the more ancient woman from Chauvet, along with the many feminine and masculine symbols represented by the signs and the art of Paleolithic caves.

• • •

Was it art for art's sake? Was it a religion or shamanism? Was it a language, or a sexual discourse? We don't know. But of all the theories that have been proposed to try to solve the continuing mystery of cave art and signs, it seems to me that the only one that is both consistent and verified by new findings is the remarkable theory of Leroi-Gourhan, based on the earlier foundation provided by Annette Laming-Emperaire.

All other theories may be seen to explain, perhaps, one aspect during one time period, based on a single depiction from a single cave—for example, the lone sorcerer from Trois Frères, which so much has been made of by the shamanism proponents—but nothing that can be verified by a preponderance of the evidence, nothing that can be supported by new findings, and nothing that is lasting or all-encompassing. Only Leroi-Gourhan's theory has all of the properties of a good, modern scientific theory.

It is perhaps ironic that science can go backward at times, when an old and discredited theory suddenly makes a comeback because a scholar in a prominent position brings it back from the dead, so to speak, ignoring its flaws and the criticisms of scholars at the time it was first proposed. In this case, however, newer is not better.

The best theory from a scientific point of view, one that has been elegantly supported by most of the evidence, one that has statistical validity, and one that is durable and can predict new findings, should once again become the reigning theory. Simply because Leroi-Gourhan's theory was proposed four decades ago does not mean we should leave it behind and follow lesser theories that have been supported less solidly by science but somehow have come into vogue.

So how should we interpret Leroi-Gourhan's findings about the Paleolithic societies that produced such rich, fascinating art and symbols? Humans were still developing culturally during the long period of the Upper Paleolithic. Having arrived in Europe from the Middle East and, before that, Africa, anatomically modern humans established themselves throughout the European continent 40,000 years ago.

Within 10,000 years or less, the last of the Neanderthals disappeared, and about that time, a little more than 30,000 years ago, the communities of anatomically modern humans in western Europe, called the Cro-Magnons, embarked on an incredible adventure of experimentation with creativity and symbolic thinking.

We don't know whether the Cro-Magnons ever reached the stage of developing a written language, although it is very likely (though unprovable) that they possessed a spoken language.

The Cro-Magnons who began to create art in caves, did develop symbolic thinking. Their great advance was to be able to reproduce artistically inside deep caves the images of animals they saw in their environment. Equally, they developed a system of signs that was also used inside these caves, in conjunction with the animals. Yet the animals depicted on cave walls and the signs that accompanied them were not random. There was a clear meaning associated with the animals and the signs.

In particular, a horse is almost always associated with a bison or an aurochs. Then, key animals such as the horse and the bison are accompanied by secondary animals such as deer or ibex. The most important discovery Leroi-Gourhan made concerns the sexual nature of the signs. According to this theory, *every* sign has one of two meanings: male or female. Thus, the language of the caves is a binary language: it has two symbols attached to it—male and female.

As such, the language could be extremely concise and powerful. It is, in a sense, an extremely advanced system of information—for we know today that *anything* can be structured in binary code. Computers and all advanced information systems in the twenty-first century are digital, meaning binary (everything is coded by strings of zeros and ones).

Of course, this is not to say that the Cro-Magnons had anything even remotely as advanced as a computing system, but the fact that their signs were binary, with every sign being male or female, gives us pause, because we know that a binary system can be immensely powerful. So, although they may not have developed a written language (or, if they had, we still have not deciphered it), they were certainly on to the essential means for information recording and transmission.

According to Leroi-Gourhan, the animals depicted on cave walls were symbols as well. Every animal, according to this theory, was itself a symbol that took on one of the two values: male or female. Thus, the bison was seen as female and the horse as male. Other animals carried similar symbolic meanings. What these meanings were, beyond their designation as gender, we do not know. But to be able to uncover the symbolic meanings of signs and pictures on cave walls was in itself a great intellectual achievement, and it is one that we should study further, rather than discount in favor of far less scientific or supportable theories about the Cro-Magnons and their culture.

We don't know what the Cro-Magnon language means, but we know it is written in binary, just like the codes that program computers and cellular phones and even the earlier Morse code used in telegraph communication, which employed dots and dashes. For the Cro-Magnons, the letters, the digits of information, were the male and female symbols. They may also have had a system of hand signals, as evidenced by hand signs found in Gargas and elsewhere. What these languages meant remains a mystery, but perhaps one that will someday be solved.

Leroi-Gourhan's idea of a code embedded in the signs—the binary code of male and female signs—certainly deserves much credit as an amazingly perceptive theory about cave art and signs, and one that should lead to further research.

But what about looking at the art itself? We in the modern Western world very rarely look at *collections* of paintings designed to be viewed together. This is not how art is produced in our world. Even if you visit an exhibition that features, say, impressionist paintings, and what you see is many paintings in the same style, this is not the same as a collection of paintings designed to be viewed as a single entity and where the environment (in this case, the walls of the exhibition) had been worked on as well, in order to create a cohesive art unit. (One exception is Monet's collection of water lily paintings from Giverny, which the artist had designed to be viewed as one entity, and which are now displayed together in the Orangerie in Paris, at the south-west corner of the Tuileries Garden.)

But that is exactly the case with cave art, which is unique in its form. It was designed to be viewed in such a way that you are not looking at one painting or one drawing by itself, but rather always seeing it within the context of all of the artworks in the cave. This, in fact, may be the reason the animals overlap. And viewed this way, the prehistoric painters may have believed they were creating harmony in the entire piece—the cave itself—when matching horses with bison and making other animal combinations that they found appealing.

Today we do not view art this way, but perhaps we should. Perhaps artists should work on larger creations that encompass several pieces. We do, however, enjoy a symphony or a play, in which many elements come together, rather than experiencing them separately. While listening to a symphony, we do not concentrate on the sound made by one instrument, but rather take in the entire harmonious production. In a play, we do not usually concern ourselves with one actor but rather are impressed by the entire production, encompassing various actors, the lighting, the stage set, the music, and other elements. Aaron Copland put this idea well in his classic book *What to Listen for in Music*:

> It is very important for all of us to become more alive to music on its sheerly musical plane. After all, an actual musical material is being used. The intelligent listener must be prepared to increase his awareness of the musical material and what happens to it. He must hear the melodies, the rhythms, the harmonies, the tone colors in a more conscious fashion. . . .
>
> Perhaps an analogy with what happens to us when we visit the theater will make this

instinctive correlation clearer. In the theater, you
are aware of the actors and actresses, costumes
and sets, sounds and movements. All these give
one the sense that the theater is a pleasant place
to be in. They constitute the sensuous plane in our
theatrical reactions. The expressive plane in the
theater would be derived from the feeling that
you get from what is happening on the stage.[6]

Perhaps the cave artists wanted us to view their grand
creations inside deep caves the way we might watch a theatrical production or listen to a classical concert. Prehistoric cave
art is a sublime art form that vanished from our world at the
end of the Ice Age and the beginning of the Neolithic with
its agriculture and urbanization. But we can still enjoy these
great artworks and thus view a form of art that has passed from
the world, and one that is unique in its form and structure, as
well as technique and harmony. We are fortunate that some
Paleolithic caves are still open to the public; people should take
advantage of the opportunity to see them. Prehistoric art is in
limited supply, and because of the potential for damage, this
opportunity may not last for long.

. . .

According to the French scholar Emmanuel Anati, the Paleolithic artists "had a vision that was absolute. [Their scenes] represent eternal truths."[7] Indeed, according to Leroi-Gourhan's and
Laming-Emperaire's theory, there is a language—a code—that is
embedded as a universal message of the cave artists. That message, hidden for posterity in the depths of almost inaccessible

caverns, is that the universe is binary: it is composed of pairs of opposing elements. These elements are represented by the horse and the bison. The two main forces of the universe are accompanied by a host of others, represented as the secondary characters in cave art: mammoths, ibex, stags, lions, rhinos, fish, and a few birds. The distinctly male and female signs that are ubiquitous in decorated caves, associated with the animals, tell the same story: our world is binary.

Whether this concept came down to us through unbroken oral and later written tradition (which is unlikely) or because we humans are hard-wired to think this way, the language of the cave artists is still with us today—although it uses a different, modern vocabulary. Today we still view the universe as binary: it is dominated by the opposing forces of male-female, light-darkness, day-night, beautiful-ugly, and good-bad. That last pair is perhaps the most meaningful. Few people view much in the human experience as gray. Every person we meet, every experience we have, we tend to classify as good or bad. There is a reason our most interesting literature is that in which a main character is both good and bad—or neither.

These truths are universal and transcend geography. Both Eastern and Western philosophy and religion partition creation into good and bad, high and low, divine and earthly, and, of course, male and female, such as the Greco-Roman pantheon with its gods and goddesses, or the Eastern deities of the two genders, balancing each other's powers.

Generally, science has taught us the same message: Electric charge is binary: positive or negative. Every action has an equal but opposite reaction (as Newton has taught us). And the universe is made of matter and antimatter—it will self-destruct if all of the matter and an equal amount of antimatter should ever meet in one location.

In fact, it is within the realm of physical science that we discover just how strongly we believe in the implicit message of the cave artists. It seems that the good-or-bad, here-or-there, male-or-female dichotomy discovered symbolically by the Cro-Magnons and then lost to the world as the Paleolithic era came to an end some 11,000 years ago is a property embedded in human consciousness. It is something that is entrenched in our minds because of our very experience on Earth. In fact, in physical realms that are foreign to our experience, different rules apply. In the micro-world of the very small, the one-quality-or-its-opposite rule breaks down immediately. An electron, for example, can be both here *and* there. The dichotomy of the cave-art code is broken in this micro-world. What rules on the microcosmic level is a very different set of commands: the language of quantum mechanics. And this language—so strange to us because we expect, as did the Cro-Magnons, a here *or* there philosophy—is accessible only to theoretical physicists who have spent decades teaching themselves a different and very unintuitive set of rules.

Equally, mathematics has been shown to explain much of the behavior patterns of the world around us. This is the mathematics of binary entities, Boolean algebra (the algebra of yes or no), which governs our computers, as well as Euclidean geometry, the concept of distance, real functions, and so on. But mathematics goes far beyond the human experience and its notions of true or false (in fact, a common mathematical method of proof, called proof by contradiction, relies on the very paradigm that a statement can be only true or false, and that no statement can hold a value that is between true or false. This method is sometimes questioned, in situations that go beyond simple logic). Mathematics extends to geometries that are non-Euclidean, to spaces that are different from ours, and to algebraic structures that defy the "normal" dichotomy discovered so long ago by the remarkable cave artists of Ice Age Europe. Situations in mathematics, philosophy, physics, or literature that fall outside of what is dictated by the binary logic that goes back to our Paleolithic past seem strange and "unreal" to us. And herein lies the profound truth encoded on the walls of deep caves so long ago.

I firmly believe that Paleolithic cave artists possessed deep understanding and perhaps even a cosmic picture of nature. Their art gives us a window through which to glimpse some of their ideas and perhaps learn something about the Cro-Magnon mind. A small number of modern experts, foremost among them Henri Breuil and André Leroi-Gourhan, have been fortunate enough to comprehend something about the sublime meaning of European cave art. And I hope that the future will bring us more intensive, serious research on Paleolithic ideas and ways of life, as seen through the art in deep caves.

Notes

2. The Greatest Mystery

1. Tattersall, p.1.
2. I owe this explanation to my editor at Wiley, Stephen Power.

4. The Roots of Language

1. See Kurlansky, p. 16.
2. Krahmalkov, p. 38

5. Abbé Breuil

1. Broderick, p. 20.
2. Ibid., p. 39.

7. The Tale of a Missing Dog

1. Broderick, p. 63.
2. Ibid., p. 65.
3. Freeman, et al., p. 75.
4. Ibid., p. 79.
5. Ibid., p. 87.

8. The Sign of the Bull and the Legend of the Minotaur

1. Mithen, p. 94.
2. Ibid., pp. 92–93.
3. Ibid., pp. 93.
4. Ibid.
5. Ibid., pp. 94–95.
6. Ibid., p. 64.

10. The Discovery of Lascaux

1. Broderick, p. 232.
2. Ibid., p. 236.
3. Mohen and Taborin, pp. 12–13. (Author's translation.)
4. Marta Falconi, "One-Horned 'Unicorn' Deer Born in Italy," *Associated Press*, June 11, 2008.

11. The Enigma of the Pit

1. Picard, pp. 252–260. (Author's translation.)
2. Bataille, *L'Éroticisme*, pp. 92–98. (Author's translation.)
3. Introduction by Stuart Kendall in Bataille, *The Cradle of Humanity*, p. 27.
4. Bataille, *The Cradle of Humanity*, pp. 50–51.

12. The Groundbreaking Work of Annette Laming-Emperaire

1. Laming-Emperaire, p. 293. (Author's translation.)
2. Ibid., p. 294.
3. Ibid.

13. Prehistoric Objets d'Art

1. Leroi-Gourhan, *Treasures of Prehistoric Art*, p. 90.
2. Delluc, p. 167.

14. The Sign of the Hand

1. Delluc, pp. 290–291. (Author's translation.)
2. Leroi-Gourhan, *Le fils du temps*, pp. 222–240. (Author's translation.)
3. Saintyves. (Author's translation.)
4. Leroi-Gourhan, *Le fils du temps*, p. 234. (Author's translation.)
5. Ibid., p. 239. (Author's translation.)

15. The Legend of the White Lady

1. Broderick, p. 252.
2. From Breuil's notes, quoted in ibid., p. 253.
3. Ibid., p. 254.
4. Clottes, *World Rock Art*, p. 10.
5. Breuil, *Four Hundred Centuries of Cave Art*, pp. 1–2.

16. Shamans of the Tundra

1. Clottes and Lewis-Williams, n. 7, p. 136. (Author's translation.)
2. See Judith Thurman, "First Impressions: What Does the World's Oldest Art Say about Us?" *New Yorker*, June 23, 2008. Thurman had interviewed Clottes while visiting the Ardèche with him.
3. Bahn, p. 63, reprinted in Clottes and Lewis-Williams, p. 158. The title of Bahn's paper contains the words "numb brain"; in their response in the reissued edition of their book in 2001, Clottes and Lewis-Williams lament that Bahn called their theory the result of a "dumb brain."
4. See Swinton, p. 22.
5. Ibid., p. 28.
6. Merkur, p. 3.
7. I refer to the shaman as "he," and indeed the shaman is male. There have been cases, however, when a shaman was a transvestite. See ibid., p. 4.
8. Ibid., p. 11.
9. Ray, p. 66.
10. Ibid., p. 66.
11. Leroi-Gourhan, *Treasures of Prehistoric Art*, p. 32.
12. Ibid., p. 34.
13. Clottes and Lewis-Williams, p. 111. (Author's translation.)
14. Ibid., p. 103.
15. Leroi-Gourhan, *Treasures of Prehistoric Art*, p. 34.
16. Leroi-Gourhan, *Les religions de la préhistoire*, p. 103. (Author's translation.)
17. Hadingham, p. 208.
18. Leroi-Gourhan, *Les religions de la préhistoire*, p. 105. (Author's translation.)

17. Stonehenge and Signs in the Sky

1. See, in particular, Alexander, pp. 34–59.
2. Ibid., p. 37.
3. Ibid., p. 38.
4. Delluc, pp. 181–182. (Author's translation.)
5. Ibid., p. 182.
6. Ibid., pp. 182–183.

18. The Mediterranean, Australia, and Patagonia

1. See the appendix by André Weil in Lévi-Strauss, pp. 257–265.
2. Lévi-Strauss, pp. 114–168 .
3. Morphy, p. 4.

19. Leroi-Gourhan's Theory

1. Leroi-Gourhan, *Le fil du temps*, p. 210. (Author's translation.)
2. Ibid. (emphasis added).
3. Ibid., p. 215.
4. Ibid.
5. Ibid., p. 216.
6. Ibid., p. 221.

20. The Relationship between Signs and Animals

1. Leroi-Gourhan, *Les religions de la préhistoire*, p. 93. (Author's translation.)
2. Ibid., p. 94.
3. Ibid., p. 102.
4. Ibid., p. 106.
5. Ibid., p. 108.
6. Ibid., p. 113.
7. Hadingham, p. 212.
8. Ibid., p. 215.
9. Ucko and Rosenfeld, p. 196.
10. Ibid., p. 200.
11. Ibid., p. 202.
12. Ibid., p. 203.
13. Ibid., p. 215.
14. Delluc, p. 284. (Author's translation.)
15. Ucko and Rosenfeld, p. 224.

21. The Chauvet Cave

1. For reasons that can only be surmised, I was unable to obtain permission from French authorities to reproduce sexually explicit images. I relied, therefore, on an excellent artist's rendering.
2. Clottes, *Chauvet Cave*, p. 168.

3. Cohen, p. 13. (Author's translation.)
4. Jung, p. 347.
5. Ibid., pp. 348–349.
6. Copland, pp. 13–14.
7. Dufay, p. 22. (Author's translation.)

References

Aujoulat, N., et al. *L'art parietal paléolithique.* Paris: Comité des Travaux Historiques et Scientifiques, 1993.

Alexander, Caroline. "If Stones Could Speak: Searching for the Meaning of Stonehenge." *National Geographic,* June 2008, pp. 34–59.

Bahn, Paul. "Membrane and Numb Brain: A Close Look at a Recent Claim for Shamanism in Paleolithic Art." *Rock Art Research* 14, no. 1 (1997): 62–68.

Bataille, Georges. *The Cradle of Humanity: Prehistoric Art and Culture.* Edited by Michelle Kendall and Stuart Kendall. New York: Zone Books, 2005.

———. *L'Éroticisme.* Paris: Minuit, 1957.

———. *Prehistoric Paintings: Lascaux or the Birth of Art.* Paris: Skira, 1955.

Breuil, Henri. *Four Hundred Centuries of Cave Art.* Montignac, France: Centre D'Études et de Documentation Préhistoriques, 1956.

Breuil, Henri, and R. Lantier. *Les hommes de la pierre ancienne.* Paris: Payot, 1959.

Broderick, Alan H. *Father of Prehistory.* New York: Morrow, 1963.

Clottes, Jean, ed. *Chauvet Cave: The Art of Earliest Times.* Translated by Paul Bahn. Salt Lake City: University of Utah Press, 2003.

———. *Grandes giraffes et fourmis vertes: Petites histoires de préhistoire.* Paris: La Maison de Roches, 2000.

———. *World Rock Art.* Los Angeles: Getty Conservation Institute, 2002.

Clottes, Jean, and David Lewis-Williams. *Les chamanes de la préhistoire.* Paris: La Maison des Roches, 2001.

Cohen, Claudine. *La femme des origins: Images de la femme dans la préhistoire occidentale.* Paris: Belin-Herscher, 2003.

Copland, Aaron. *What to Listen for in Music.* New York: Signet, 2002.

De Beaune, Sophie A. *Les Hommes au temps de Lascaux: 40000–10000 avant J.-C.* Paris: Hachette, 1995.

Delluc, Gilles. *Le sexe au temps des Cro-Magnons.* Périgueux: Pilote 24, 2006.

Dufay, François. "Ce que nous dit l'art des caverns." Cover article, *L'Express,* August 14, 2008, p. 22.

Freeman, L. G., with J. Gonzales Echegaray, F. Bernaldo de Quiros, and J. Ogden. *Altamira Revisited and Other Essays on Early Art.* Chicago: Institute for Prehistoric Investigations, 1987.

Hadingham, Evan. *Secrets of the Ice Age: The World of the Cave Artists.* New York: Walker, 1979.

Johnson, R. Townley. *Major Rock Paintings of Southern Africa.* Bloomington: Indiana University Press, 1979.

Jung, Carl G. *Man and His Symbols.* New York: Dell, 1968.

Krahmalkov, Charles R. *A Phoenician-Punic Grammar.* Boston: Brill, 2001.

Kurlansky, Mark. *The Basque History of the World.* New York: Vintage, 2001.

Laming-Emperaire, Annette. *La signification de l'art rupestre paléolithique: Methodes et applications.* Paris: Picard, 1962.

Leroi-Gourhan, André. *Le fil du temps.* Paris: Fayard, 1983.

———. *Les religions de la préhistoire.* Paris: Quadrige/PUF, 1964.

———. *Treasures of Prehistoric Art.* New York: Abrams, 1967.

Lévi-Strauss, Claude. *Les structures élémentaires de la parenté.* New York: Mouton de Gruyter, 2002.

Lewis-Williams, David. *The Mind of the Cave.* London: Thames and Hudson, 2002.

Merkur, Dan. *Becoming Half Hidden: Shamanism and Initiation among the Inuit.* New York: Garland, 1992.

Mithen, Steven. *After the Ice.* Cambridge, MA: Harvard University Press, 2004.

Mohen, J. P., and Y. Taborin. *Les Sociétés de la Préhistoire*. Paris: Hachette, 2005.

Morphy, Howard. *Aboriginal Art*. London: Phaidon, 1998.

Peyrony D. "La Ferrassie." *Préhistoire* 3 (1934): 1–92.

Picard, Jacques J. *Le Mythe Fondateur de Lascaux*. Paris: L'Harmattan, 2003.

Ray, Dorothy Jean. *Eskimo Art: Tradition and Innovation in North Alaska*. Seattle: University of Washington Press, 1977.

Saintyves, P. "La main dans la magie." *Aesculape*, March 3, 1934.

Sandars, N. K. *Prehistoric Art in Europe*. New York: Penguin, 1968.

Sieveking, Ann. *The Cave Artists*. London: Thames and Hudson, 1979.

Swinton, George. *Eskimo Sculpture*. Toronto: McClelland and Stewart, 1965.

Tattersall, Ian. *Becoming Human: Evolution and Human Uniqueness*. New York: Harcourt, 1998.

Thurman, Judith. "First Impressions: What Does the World's Oldest Art Say about Us?" *New Yorker*, June 23, 2008.

Torbrügge, Walter. *Prehistoric European Art*. New York: Abrams, 1968.

Ucko, Peter J., and Andrée Rosenfeld. *Paleolithic Cave Art*. New York: McGraw-Hill, 1967.

Illustration Credits

Table of signs: pp. 61, 63, 64, 78, 79, 99, 183, 188, 208, Thomas Barron.

Photo insert credits: plates 1, 2, 4, Debra Gross Aczel; plate 3, Marie-Odile and Jean Plassard; plates 5, 6, French Ministry of Culture and Communication, Direction de L'Architecture et du Patrimoine; plates 7, 8, Wikimedia Foundation, Inc.; plates 9, 10, 11, 12, 13, 14, 15, French Ministry of Culture and Communication, Direction Régionale des Affaires Culturelles Rhône-Alpes; plate 16, Thomas Barron.

Index

Page numbers in *italics* refer to illustrations.

Henry (Jung's psychoanalysis patient),
212–213
Hodder, Ian, 67
Homo antecessor ("Pioneer Man"), 29
Homo erectus, 29–30, 37
Homo heidelbergensis, 19–20, 29
Homo neanderthalensis, 19, 32, 37.
See also Neanderthals
Homo sapiens, 19, 37
horses
dotted horses of Pech Merle, *76,*
76–77, 80, 81, 153–154
as gender representation, 142,
186–191, 193–205, 211
Horse Sector of Chauvet cave, *141,*
209, 210
House, Julie, 173–174
houses (Neolithic), images on walls of,
65–68
Hoxne, England, 20–21
human figures, as cave art subject, 103
hunting
Breuil on, 17, 86, 94–98, 99–100
Paleolithic diet and, 155, 195
Pit of Lascaux and, *94,* 94–98, *99,*
99–100
Hunting Lions (panel, Chauvet cave),
141, *141*
hyoid bone, 35

Ice Age, 4, 9, 11
indicative panels, 73, 184, 189
Inuit religion, 149–151
Iraq, 26
Israel (cave names)
Amud, 31
Kebara, 31
Qafzeh, 30, 31
Skhul, 30, 31
Tabun, 25–26, 30–31
Italy, 8, 171

Java, 37
"Java Man," 30
Jericho, 65
Jochman, Hugo, 123–124
Johanson, Donald, 36

Jordan Valley, 65, 66
Jumping Cow, The (Lascaux cave), 89
Jung, Carl, 212–213

Kakadu National Park (Australia), 177
Kalahari, 143
Kebara (Mt. Carmel cave), 31
Kendall, Stuart, 96
King, William, 22, 32
Knossos, Crete, 68–70, 127
Konya Plain, 66
Kuzshuktuk (Eskimo shaman), 150

Labyrinth, 68–69
La Chaffaud (cave), 107
La Chapelle-aux-Saints (cave), 32
Lagarde, Fernand, 189
La Madeleine (rock), 27, 28, 48, 56, 108
La Marche (rock), 111–112
Laming-Emperaire, Annette, 63–64, 91,
99–106, 179–180, 201, 203, 204
La Mouthe (cave), 48–49
language, 35–40
Azilian rocks and, 43–44
cave art as binary code and, 215–221
symbolic thinking and, 27, 35–36
La Pasiega (cave), 201–202
Lascaux (cave), 18–19, 50, 59, 186
discovery of, 83–91
diverticulum (Axial Gallery), 87,
88–89
dots in, 157–158, 163
The Great Bull, 89, 89–91
licorne of, 103
Nave of, 85
Pit of, 85, 93–98, *94, 99*
Rotunda (Hall of the Bulls), 88
sections of, 87–91
Last Glacial Maximum (LGM), 18
Laussel, France. *See Venus with the
Horn, The* (rock engraving)
La Vache (dwelling cave), 108
Laval, Léon, 84
Le Moustier, France, 28, 48
Lemozi, Amédée, 76
lemurs, 15
Le Portel (cave), 202